# Praise for

*"You had me at 'Perfection is a Myth.' I couldn't agree with that more and am thrilled that Luke is sounding the drum about creativity, God and what it means to have a calling."*

**Jon Acuff**
New York Times Bestselling Author
of *Finish, Give Yourself the Gift of Done*

*"If you've ever thought about starting an organization, creating something from scratch, or bringing a new idea to life, you'll love this book! I find the story of SALT to be inspiring, uplifting, and challenging because of Luke McElroy. He's the real deal!"*

**Clay Scroggins**
Lead Pastor, North Point Community Church

*"Luke writes with a spirit of humility and winsomeness, inviting his readers to go on a journey that explores the creative process in light of Scripture and practical wisdom. I urge you to take that journey with Luke and see what God stirs up in you!"*

**Nancy Beach**
Former Programming Director,
Willow Creek Community Church

*"If you've ever thought you have some God-given creative gifts, this book is a must read! I've seen first hand these principles at work in the lives of so many who have attended SALT Conference over the years."*

**Jeremy Cowart**
World Renowned Photographer & Entrepreneur

# CREATIVE POTENTIAL

## PRINCIPLES FOR UNLEASHING YOUR GOD-GIVEN CALLING

**LUKE MCELROY**

FOREWORD BY GARY MOLANDER

Published in Nashville, Tennessee through SALT Conferences, a division of Orange Thread Media, LLC. For bulk, educational or organizational licenses, please contact SALT Conferences for pricing and details at www.SALTcommunity.com.

Cover Design: Nick Rivero and Jacob Blaze
Book Layout: Douglas Williams and Luke McElroy
Edited by: Katie Strandlund and Heather Ebert

Paperback ISBN: 978-0-9913307-4-4
Library of Congress Control Number: 2018932161

FOR THE CORE.

(YOU KNOW WHO YOU ARE)

# CONTENTS

# FOREWORD

Luke McElroy and I live in opposite ends of the United States—Tennessee and California, to be more precise. So when I discovered that I would be in Nashville on business for a few days in 2012, it provided us with an easy excuse to get together. But I never would have predicted what Luke would share in our time together.

You and I and everyone else on the planet experience the calling of God in different ways, at different levels, and with different responses. Some of us hear His voice calling to us through the voices of other people, while others hear it more through the voice of our own hearts. For some people, hearing Christ accurately requires a certain amount of personal brokenness and suffering at the time, while others seem to hear Him with confidence and boldness, almost like a text message or voicemail. Some of us run toward the invitation, while others spend our lives running away from it, and always with a believable excuse.

Regardless of how we experience the calling of God, make no mistake that when He invites us to do something, it's a big guttural roar that elicits fear and reverence, but also one that speaks softly to us with words we've been created to hear ever since our hearts' first beat.

The calling of God whispers with thunder.

As Luke and I sat down for dinner at one of those restaurants furthering Nashville's foodie scene, Luke was experiencing the call of God in every way possible.

God was whispering to Luke, and it felt like thunder.

The message was surprising to me, but I never told him that, mostly because I didn't want to dampen this twenty-something's enthusiasm. When I was in my twenties, I had several mentors who dampened my enthusiasm to change the world, and I never want to do that to anyone. Luke told me that God was calling him to create a conference.

A conference.

And what I really mean to say is, "Are you sure about this? Another conference?"

You already know this, but I'll just say it—there are so many conferences available to people, each with their own spin messaging and target audience. All seem to promise something that may or may not be fulfilled, and a few appear to serve the conference coordinator more than the blessed attendees who have convinced their senior pastor that this is a good stewarding of the church's budget.

But this conference was different, and that's because Luke is different. Luke is equal parts desperate entrepreneur, starving artist, and loving shepherd. And as we continued to experience life across the table that evening, Luke spoke with enough passion to make me listen, and with enough fear to make me believe.

The conference would be called SALT, and the SALT leadership team would equip media folks in churches who serve behind the scenes weekly. Technicians, artists, pastors, designers, worship leaders and videographers would hit pause from serving their church for three days, and instead allow themselves to be served.

It would be a highly practical conference, but one that took aim directly at the overworked and under resourced heart of each person in attendance. Most conferences choose a practical how-to emphasis or a heart emphasis. Luke wanted to do both.

Eighteen months later, we gathered in a back room of the conference venue site, getting ready to pray and ask God to make Himself known to everyone at this inaugural event. Luke began to speak, but after only a few words, he broke down crying. I don't remember any other words spoken during that moment, because I was too busy experiencing the desperation of a young man who was surrendering everything of any importance into the hands of the only One who could handle the full weight of his desperation.

He said "Amen," and five minutes later we appeared on the main stage together, welcoming people to the first-ever SALT Conference.

That was four conferences ago.

In the coming pages, you'll experience the journey I was invited into at that table in Nashville, and you'll likely find your own story as Luke reveals all that God was doing in that season. You'll also experience the heart of what was taught at those conferences—not as a conference capture or repeat, but as timeless principles our tribe needs to hear and see and implement.

This is where feel-good worship meets an exhausting, drenching sweat.

This is where time-tested principles meet a timeless Mystery.

This is where walking and running and dancing come together, and where all forms of creativity are given life by the Giver of all creativity.

And this is where your own creative calling comes into clear view, not because God needs you to exert your creativity, but because the world is crying out for you to.

So as you read these pages, I pray that you make your heart open and available and willing. I pray that you see new things in old ways, and old things in new ways. I pray that the brilliance of Christ is displayed to you, in you, for the sake of the world.

And I pray that as God whispers to you, He does so—with thunder.

**— Gary Molander,**
Author of *Pursuing Christ, Creating Art*
and Founder of Floodgate Productions.

# PRELUDE

January 29, 1995. That was *my* Sunday. The Sunday I gave my life to Christ. A day I have never forgotten.

Growing up in a discipleship-focused church, there's an unspoken plan to becoming a follower of Christ. First you likely pray the "prayer," immediately followed by filling out a card, and eventually you meet with a youth leader or pastor. In that meeting, you begin to explore God's will for your life. The hope is to walk out with clarity on your "call from God," and how to make the most of your life for the kingdom of God.

Being a son to two parents who had been Christians nearly their entire lives as well, I guess it didn't surprise me that God had a purpose for my life. Being a McElroy, it was somewhat implied. You're going to be asked by God to do something amazing with your life.

Maybe I was naive. Hopefully it was just my age. But I thought I would get a literal phone call from God. Looking back now, I can only laugh at that concept, as you likely did reading that sentence. But several areas of the Christian faith didn't make much sense to me back then, so I guess I just had that *childlike* faith to think my phone would ring. Writing this now, I realize how often I tell myself that God is this incredibly understandable being. But in doing so, I am merely diminishing the wonder, mystery, and beauty His presence radiates.

Part of me is convinced that God doesn't want to be fully understood. Knowledge is power, and power in the wrong hands can lead to complete destruction. I don't say this to imply that God's intent for mankind is to be dumb or naive, but maybe He delights in our reliance on Him for the answers to most of life's biggest questions.

It's why I believe there's celestial joy in our being like a child when it comes to our faith. Over the years I've begun to see the difference between a childish faith and a childlike faith, and God loves the childlike faith because children have such an amazing ability to trust and believe the impossible and to take God at His word.

As our minds develop and we grow out of our childhood, our faith leaves the embrace of the impossible and begins to doubt the uncertain.

What you're about to read is a story. My story. A story of how my own creative potential was unleashed as I began to trust God at His word and recognize that His will guides my path. This is a story of learning how to operate out of the creative calling that God has purposed for each and every one of His children.

It's a story of hearing the call from God and stepping into the wonder of the unknown as I ventured toward my role in God's greater story. But as you read, I hope you don't just read my story, but find your own story among the pages to follow. And you begin to see that God is ready to unlock your own creative and divine potential as well.

As you make your way into the second act, I'll spend the remaining chapters breaking down the four principles that will help you maximize your creative potential. Through this portion of the book, I'll share strategies, biblical insights, and relatable stories to help make it as practical as possible to step into your God-given calling with the confidence of the cross behind you. As Paul writes in Galatians 5:1, "It is for freedom that Christ has set us free." This freedom he talks about includes the purpose God has given you, so run with the confidence of freedom and the guarantee of the resurrection as you unleash your potential.

However, before you begin this first act and begin to read the narrative of God's handiwork on my life, I want to ask of you one thing: be willing.

I know that sounds all lofty and super spiritual, however that's not my intent. It's not my intent to be one of those authors to set you on an emotional roller-coaster either. Because an emotional rollercoaster isn't the core of my story.

As all our stories do, what you're about to read involves some pain and some joy. Some going and some stopping. Some faith and some failure. But as I learned to let go of control, pride, and my own stubborn will, I found that I wasn't losing anything. I was letting go, letting myself grow, and growing closer to God in the process.

With God, I've found that the more you give, the more you gain. It's completely paradoxical to the world. But it's what makes God so mysteriously beautiful to me. As you will read in the story to follow, the more I filled my life with the presence and person of Jesus Christ, the more my art, my creativity, and essentially my calling began to impact the world.

Maybe you have already had *your Sunday*. And you've begun the amazing journey of waiting for the call God has on your life. Maybe this is just another book in a series of books you thought you were supposed to read as you increase your faith.

I hope it isn't just *another* book though. Because for me, I dove head first into the knowledge of God before I understood the heart of God. I now know that is being childish, not childlike, with my faith.

In some crazy way, I believed that reading everything I could on the Christian lifestyle would help me find the phone number for God so I could speed up the waiting process and get that providential call from God. Here's what I've found though: there is no Fast Pass in the kingdom of God like there is in the Magic Kingdom at Disney World.

Some days I wish I had the ability to go back in time and tell my teenage self to be more willing in the waiting. But most days I'm grateful for the story He wrote for my life. I'm grateful for the insights He continually shows me about my own potential in this life, even to this day, decades after *my Sunday*.

But I'm getting ahead of myself. I need to get back to the beginning.

Welcome to Act I.

# ACT I

## CHAPTER ONE

# Calling, Camps, and CEOs

The day I heard God's call on my life wasn't out of the ordinary. The voice of James Earl Jones wasn't present, telling me to do something. In fact, there wasn't a single audible word. When God speaks, your heart and soul know who's speaking. That call would soon bear fruit, and eventually change the outcome of my entire life. And I would recognize my potential as I created out of the divine overflow in my life.

I don't know what sort of youth group you were a part of growing up. Maybe you didn't attend youth group growing up. But I did. Not only did I attend youth group, I was offered an internship with my youth pastor the summer of my senior year in high school.

Ever since I can remember, our youth pastor took trips to Panama City Beach, Florida, with our middle school and high school ministries. We filled dozens of chartered buses, the ones that pull into Greyhound stations every day, and gave hundreds of parents a week off as we took their students to beach camp. It was always a highlight of my summers growing up.

However, this specific year I wasn't attending as a student. It was my last year at beach camp, and I was the intern. One of my responsibilities was to make sure the sugar-crazed middle school students didn't get too rambunctious or injure themselves before we got to the emerald waters of the Gulf Coast.

The bus had those cloth seats with that '80s rainbow-colored, vertical pattern. Maybe this was to cover the stains from Snickers Bars that wouldn't make it entirely into a student's mouth or the Skittles thrown from row to row. Eventually the Skittles and Snickers became one with the cloth, and it became obvious that the rainbow pattern was designed to camouflage the sugar that fused with the seats.

So there I was. Sitting toward the front of a bus packed with a loud group of middle and high school students, headed once again to beach camp. There wasn't much to drown out the noise of all the students. Netflix didn't exist back then, so there was no binge-watching another television show to drown out the adolescent chaos that ensued behind me.

My choices were reading a book or listening to my Sony Walkman. But back then, your music player required AA batteries, and mine had just run out. I couldn't focus on reading, so I chose to let my mind wander as I watched the white dashed lines pass by on the road beneath.

Crazy concept to just let your mind wander, isn't it? The idea of just letting your brain think for a moment, and not be so consumed with the latest app or social media feed? But it was the early 2000s, and I didn't have a device with the world at my fingertips.

It was in that wandering, gazing out of the window that I felt God drop a picture into my mind. One with stunning clarity and amazing detail.

The location of the picture was unknown. It was a room, and I was standing in the back, with a crowd of people in front of me. The people in the picture had their hands lifted high in the air. It was likely this was a worship service. And it seemed to me that people were *unhindered* by the glory of God and the centrality of the Cross.

As I began to focus on this picture more and more, something stood out to me—the room wasn't full of ordinary people. Instead, it was clear that God wanted me to see that these worshipers "didn't understand their influence in the world." And in this picture, I too was among this same group.

Maybe I was in the back of the room so God could give me perspective. Maybe I was in the back because I too had not recognized my influence in the world. Or maybe I was in the back because it somehow connected with my role in the story I felt God was inviting me into in this moment.

As I looked out among this mass of people, before me was the trajectory of my life. One day, I believed, I would see this picture before my very own eyes.

Quickly it came, quickly it vanished. Much like a time-lapse film of traffic in a major city. The blur of a moment, but an imprint that was forever stamped on my life.

It was one of those moments you wish you could grab the remote of your life and click the rewind button, as if our lives were DVR systems on our TV. But reality doesn't allow that, and all I was left with was a whisper in visual form. A whisper I'd never forget.

## A Flood of Questions

Immediately, I was immersed in an ocean of questions. On one hand, I was preoccupied with the curiosity of what would come while drowning in the fear of the unknown.

Who were the people in the room? What were their names? Did they come from a specific city or church? Was it even a church? In fear, I wondered if this was what it feels like when God says to go plant a church, but I was certain that wasn't what He was saying.

These people, what was their story? What was my involvement? When would this "event" take place? Was it an "event"? When should I start planning? Would I need money? Do I know anyone who has a lot of money? What is a lot of money? Who else would be involved in this dream?

As the questions began to overwhelm me, I resolved to one simple plea: "Lord, please give me details!"

I wanted so desperately to seek clarity on the call I seemed to have just received. My heart was pounding out of my chest. Adrenaline was running high. There wasn't a word in the world that would have adequately expressed my level of excitement.

I was ready to start.

Ready to do *something*. To get working on this nearly impossible task of creating this moment! This was *the call* from God, and I was stuck on a fifty-five-passenger, Skittle-infused, rainbow-patterned bus, headed to the

beach with a bunch of middle schoolers high on sugar—
the worst!

## God's Starting Gate

Have you ever seen a horse race? They put the horses
in a mobile stall called a *starting gate,* also known as a
starting barrier, and it's designed to ensure a fair start
for the race. Once the horse is loaded into its respective
stall, the back side is shut and locked in place. The only
way out is through the starting gate.

The announcer makes a few statements to get the
crowd excited. Anticipation increases and the starting
pistol is fired! Simultaneously, the gates open and the
horses take off. But my starting gate door was jammed.
That's at least how it felt, having this call from God while
stuck on this bus headed to the beach. I couldn't start.
Stalled by the lock of a door I couldn't pry open.

In all actuality, I was nowhere near the starting gate
of God's purpose for my life. In fact, I wasn't even at the
racetrack or about to enter the gate into the warm-up
pen. I was in a pasture, out in the middle of nowhere, and
it wasn't my turn to begin running quite yet.

It's amazing how backward I allowed that moment to
become. Looking back now, with almost 20/20 vision, I
can see that I tried to insert a worldly principle of "work
hard or die trying" into a God-ordained purpose. I was
trying to pry the stuck starting gate because I thought
it was my duty to start running. As if somewhere in the
Bible it stated that success in God's eyes is only achieved
by forward progress at an unprecedented rate.

I wanted to get off that bus and start forging the path toward re-creating that picture. But I've learned in my life that the more I try to control my own story, the more of God's glory I inevitably steal. God gets the greatest glory from my story when I'm most on His timing.

Israel Houghton, songwriter and former worship leader for Lakewood Church in Houston, Texas, once said, "Don't ask God to provide you a horse so you can learn how to ride it. Instead, learn how to ride horses and God will provide a horse to ride."

So often in my own life, I allow the passion of my purpose to overshadow the preparation *for* my purpose. It's as if the excitement of a new idea blinds me from seeing the need to be taught, mentored, trained, and prepared before I start. No true craftsman ever gets to where they are without proper training and an immense amount of time. I wanted to run. But God wasn't asking me to start the race as much as He was asking me to start the training.

When God calls you to something, you better believe it's going to be so that you can become the best. It's never His intent that you would be merely mediocre at something, but that you would excel, so He can get the glory in your story.

My mistake was that I didn't believe God would do the work. I thought that was up to me. So here I was asking God for a horse, when I needed to be waiting for Him to show me how to ride a horse first. My own willpower got in the way.

God has always been a map maker. But I've found He doesn't just create the map and leave me to explore on my own. He wants to be my guide in the exploration too!

God never intended for us to be self-guided sojourners in the pursuit of His purpose for our lives.

God doesn't settle. When God chooses someone to fill a role in His kingdom, you better believe they're going to be His first choice. His prized protégé. God's top pick for the job.

Nothing is an overnight success. Nothing. But being younger and new to this whole God thing, I got caught up in the serendipity that God wanted this picture to become an instant reality. However, that wasn't at all the case.

Just because a no-name author can instantly become a *New York Times* best seller, or some business is seemingly making millions on the NYSE, doesn't mean it was as instant as you or I may have observed. Too often I forget that before any public praise, there will be a season of incredible private preparation.

God doesn't need me to fulfill His purposes in the world. He *wants* me to play a part in His story. Instead of being an invitation to the destination in that picture God gave me, He was inviting me to private preparation. So I may have been moving, on a bus to the beach, but God had some work to do first.

Just as an artist uses a chisel on wood to create a beautiful sculpture, God was about to chip away some unnecessary elements of my own character and giftedness. He was about to turn me into the beautiful work of art that He purposed from the beginning of time. With God, some things must go before they can grow. In this season, I knew God was using the chisel on my life, to make room for the things He was wanting to make new and renew. This was a process that took humility, time and a lot of faith.

While I was stuck behind a gate that wouldn't open, trying to pry my way into a race I wasn't ready to run, God was teaching me a profound lesson. Don't try to microwave God's call on your life when His intent might be to use a slow cooker.

## Prying the Gates Open

The days became weeks and weeks became months as I waited for answers to my questions. As time progressed, I seemed to choose my own answers to the questions. You should know that I'm very driven. If God said go, and the starting gate didn't open, I'd eventually figure out how to get that gate open.

The more questions I processed, the more answers I made up. And the more answers I gave myself, the more self-defined my calling became. I took this holy and sacred picture from God and began doing my own Photoshop work by adding elements here and there to provide *answers* to the questions I was beckoning.

Though I didn't see it at the time, the clearer the picture became for me, the more distant it was from God. I was hand-prying that gate open with a life-size crowbar. Eventually I pried enough to allow me to escape this delayed start to the perceived race.

As I started running, oblivious to the fact that I was on my own racetrack, I made a pretty definitive decision about that picture I had been Photoshopping.

The picture was a youth camp.

The people I saw *had to be* students, middle schoolers and high schoolers. And the reason they had their hands in the air worshiping is in response to a worship song that was playing. So I added a stage and placed a youth minister into my Photoshop canvas.

Since I had already taken liberties of my own on defining this picture from God, I had to keep going. The camp needed a theme. It had to have a name. There was staff to recruit and a lake with a blob to be built. The list of details that would make this picture a reality went on and on.

This dream to build a camp consumed my every thought. And in my own ambition, I ran with a never-before-seen intensity, designing every detail and strategizing every element.

I thought of a name. The name became a logo. The logo became a domain name. The domain name became a beautiful website. That website became the vehicle to start fundraising.

I dreamed. I dreamed again. I identified key roles and my ideal staff. I prayed that staff would quit their jobs. And work for me.

I planned. I procured details. I researched as much as I could. I spent nearly every waking minute working on this camp.

One afternoon, not long after beach camp was over, I found myself speaking to a lawyer about how to file and register for a 501(c)3 nonprofit status. I set up a meeting with a real estate agent to inquire about the cost per acre of land in North Georgia, you know—for the lake and the blob.

I came up with camp themes and designed posters that advertised those themes. I researched other camp organizations and wrote out strategies of how we were going to be *different*. I even called some of my parent's friends. They needed time to start thinking about how much they were going to donate once we had our 501(c)3 nonprofit status ready and they could get a tax deduction.

It's funny to reflect on all of this now and realize how much my prayer life shifted during this process. In the beginning my prayers were massive questions about what God was trying to tell me, seeking the purpose of this picture. However, as the months went on and on, my prayer life became a quest for clarity on all the tiniest of details.

Everyone who knew me knew I wanted to start a camp, and most of them believed I would one day. I found myself sharing the vision of this camp with my friends, parent's friends, youth pastor, church volunteers, and almost anyone who was older than me and knew how to breathe. (As if age plus breathing meant potential financial partner.)

## A Camp for CEOs

For the next eighteen months, I jumped all-in toward planning the creation of a youth camp. The vision: help students see their influence in the world for kingdom purposes.

I became empowered by this concept that to reach the world for the sake of Christ, we wouldn't need an abundance of preachers, pastors, and missionaries. Instead, we would need an abundance of people who had significant cultural influence and changed the world by the communities they were shaping. If I could help students see the potential of gaining more influence in the world, then help them on their path toward discipleship, the world would be radically changed for the sake of the kingdom of God.

I began to study the *Fortune* magazine list of the five hundred most successful companies. This list was known as the Fortune 500 and became the measuring stick of the potential impact future students could (and would) have on culture. My vision was to see the Fortune 500 full of God-fearing men and women because of this camp experience.

If this camp could become a launching pad for the future CEOs of the world, we would have our hand on developing assets for the kingdom of God that would have monumental impact on society at large. And if the men and women on that list were God-fearing, Christ-proclaiming, Spirit-empowered individuals, the earth would be covered in the presence of God's providential grace and love.

Essentially I started to build a camp for future CEOs and Kid Presidents. I imagined that this camp could become a place that would prepare them not only for the business world of managing people, raising capital, innovating great ideas, and leading mighty enterprises for cultural good, but could also provide a spiritual and theological foundation for their lives.

Here's what's ironic about this idea: it's a great idea that has a lot of potential to impact the kingdom of God.

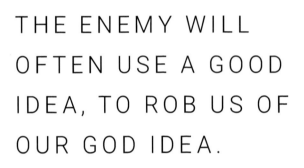

THE ENEMY WILL
OFTEN USE A GOOD
IDEA, TO ROB US OF
OUR GOD IDEA.

#CREATIVEPOTENTIAL

It's not that it lacked a kingdom vision or Christ-centered perspective that made it not right for me to pursue. It just wasn't the idea God had purposed me to pursue. In fact, this camp still needs to be built! It would likely have an incredible impact on the expansion of Jesus's fame in all of the world. The enemy will often use a good idea to rob us of our God idea.

The picture God had for me wasn't a camp, and I'm so glad that I recognized that early in my story. When I went back to that picture, confident that it was a vision from God, I started to identify the difference between that good idea and the God idea! Lucky for me, my youth pastor was one of many I had told about the youth camp. He was the exact person God used to help me realize I was prying open the wrong gate, and I was getting in the way of my true purpose, which meant I wasn't anywhere near the potential God had in store. When we know our potential is before us, the waiting isn't waiting, it's preparing, and our compass begins to realign heavenward.

## CHAPTER TWO

# A Wall and Three Questions

In January of my senior year in high school, my youth pastor, Drew, suggested a book that would change the trajectory of my life.

Drew was very aware of the calling I had proclaimed over my life of starting a youth camp. The book he gave me was *Visioneering: God's Blueprint for Developing and Maintaining Vision* by Andy Stanley.

In *Visioneering*, Andy shares the story of the biblical character Nehemiah and his journey to rebuild the wall surrounding Jerusalem. Nehemiah wanted to protect the temple from an attack by an opposing country or enemy. Throughout the book, Andy uncovers the tension that lives in every leader who is called into something far bigger than themselves, and within the pages he details the way in which we respond to that call in our daily lives.

As I was reading, chapters 1 through 6 became encouragement for my vision to build a youth camp. In fact, the fifth chapter has this line: "Faith is confidence that God is who he says he is and that he will do what he has promised to do."[1] It reminded me so much of one of my favorite scriptures in the New Testament, 1

Thessalonians 5:24, where the apostle Paul writes: "The one who calls you is faithful, and he will do it."

The problem wasn't that I lacked faith, but that in reading this book, I realized the faith I had was in the wrong place. To others, they may have perceived that my "faith" was in God, when it was a "faith" in myself. In other words, ego.

I recognized that in this process of chasing a call from God, I put my hope and excitement on *self*-confidence in a *self*-prescribed plan, rather than on *God*-confidence in a *God*-ordained plan.

For as long as I can remember, I was the one who wanted to make things happen in life. I have an insatiable desire to see forward progress on a project. The problem with a desire so focused on always trying to accomplish the impossible is that it led me to need a plan to get things done over a pursuit of the Provider who guides my steps. That's a dangerous place to be.

When our love for our calling overshadows our love for our Creator, the focus of our lives shift from *being* to *doing*. God never defines our value using a list of things we've done or the things we will one day do. Yes, we all have amazing potential to *do* great things, but first and foremost, God is madly in love with who we are and the person we are *becoming* in relationship with Him!

The very first prayer I had when I saw that picture, riding on that bus to Panama City Beach, Florida, was "God, is this your will?" and I quickly began praying, "God, what is the next step?" In that bus, I never realized that my prayer started in a place of who I was becoming in light of the purposes of God, rather than the tasks that were before me. A shift from being to doing. And that tiny degree of change, which was seemingly unnoticeable in the moment, changed the trajectory of the journey I would embark on.

It's amazing how soon we go from wanting to know God's will for our life to wanting to know every detail of our way for our life. And what God intended to be a relational journey *with* Him quickly becomes a pursuit absent of Him. Our only interactions are when we're asking God to bless the plans we came up with.

There is a realization I came to a few years ago as I was reflecting on this portion of my story. God blesses the things He ordains. It's against His character not to! When we must ask God to bless something, it may be an indicator light going off that we may have concocted our own plan for our lives, or we've deviated slightly off course.

When we seek the *way* of God, we merely seek a process. In doing so, our focus is on our doing. The result is a relationship where God requires a list of to-dos, tasks, and steps to encounter His presence. To me, that's religion. Not relationship.

Though it took me months, I realized the powerful part of the Nehemiah story. Yes, God wanted to use Nehemiah to *do* something, but more importantly, God wanted Nehemiah to *be* something. God experienced intimacy with Nehemiah, more than just a transaction where Nehemiah asks for a set of directions and God hands them over. Therefore, Nehemiah is an amazing man of God because he was both faithful to God's plan and faithful to God Himself.

It's so easy to get the love for Creator and our love for calling out of proportion, isn't it? Because as an artist, engineer, architect, creative, or craftsman, we get so caught up in the details of our calling, forgetting who called us into it in the first place. It was as if the lightbulb had switched on as I continued to study Nehemiah. The story wasn't about a wall; it was about God's will for his life!

Yes, Nehemiah was being asked to build something, but God was way more concerned with the process than the product. In the end, the same was true for me and this plan to build a camp.

Let me say it again. God is more concerned about the process than the product. Not because of our doing that takes place in a process but because of the person we become in relationship with Christ through a process.

So I put *Visioneering* down.

And with it I laid down the picture God had given me. The Photoshop window I so eagerly tweaked to near perfection in my head needed to be closed.

## The Beauty in Waiting

For nearly all of life I've wrestled with waiting. Being someone who loves to see results, make stuff happen, and work with an unhealthy intensity, I so easily believe success lies within the doing. I got so caught up in doing something for God that I missed the process to become something by God. And there's a big difference in those two things.

Think about it this way. God can *do* anything in the entire world. He made the earth in six days. Who am I to think that He needs me to *do* anything?

GOD IS MORE
CONCERNED ABOUT
PROCESS THAN THE
PRODUCT.

#CREATIVEPOTENTIAL

My life was designed with incredible purpose to do amazing things. But my pride has been the wall that prevents me from reaching my potential over and over. It was my pride that caused me to want to control my picture of the purpose in my life. It was my pride that was so obsessed with doing over being, and therefore, it was my pride that I needed to lay down.

Laying down my pride hurt, because for the first time since that Skittle-infused, rainbow-patterned bus ride, I had let go of the steering wheel on the direction of my life. I look back now and see the purpose in that season, but back then it felt like I had come to a place of complete purposelessness, just spinning my tires. It felt as if the tires had spun for so long with no traction that the car overheated and quit running altogether.

As I write this, I wish I had a way to write a letter to my high school self. It would simply say this:

> Dear Luke,
>
> Don't fret the details right now, for there's incredible beauty in the waiting! Instead be willing. Willing to give. Because with God, giving is gaining.
>
> Soon you will embark on a preparation process that will bring you and God closer than you could ever imagine. That relational intimacy will bring you far more love, peace, purpose, and strength than you will find in the hustle of doing by yourself.
>
> From the future,
>
> — L.

I think the reason Isaiah uses the image of the pot and the clay in Isaiah 64:8 is to help us see why waiting is part of God's plan for our lives. When the potter is molding the clay, he keeps adding a substantive amount of water. This is a grueling process for the potter, as they exert energy pushing, pulling, and shaping the new mold, all the while spinning on the potter's wheel. Once completed, the potter places it into a high temperature furnace. And it sits. In the heat.

Over time, this high temperature environment causes all the water added during the molding process to evaporate, allowing the clay to become a hard, stone-like material. It's a curing process that can't be rushed and can take hours upon hours.

Just because God had shown me the shape I was to become with my life didn't mean I was ready to be the container God designed me for. Because I still had to dry out. After putting Andy Stanley's book down, I entered a new season, one where I was to enter the fiery furnace. I felt the heat because there was pressure from those around me to continue building the camp. There was also social pressure. In many ways, I felt I had let my friends and family down by giving up the camp idea.

Every so often, I'd check myself to see if I was ready to be taken out of the furnace. But then I'd see an area that was still "wet," and I'd recognize that it was just me wanting to control again. So I'd just sit back and let the fire continue to do its curing.

Waiting isn't easy, as I don't think it's designed to be. But waiting is a requirement for almost anything that's worthwhile, because it reminds us that life isn't about that thing or ourselves. So there I was in a new season of life, the beautiful wait.

It may have looked like I had hit the pause button on God's call on my life. I may have felt like I hit the stop button instead. But I can see now that, by entering the season of the beautiful wait, I was pressing the play button on the true calling that God had for me. It wasn't the play button on what I was going to *do* but the relationship I would soon gain with God.

## The Waiting Game and a New Name

Life in the beautiful wait can be a bit mundane and quite repetitive. I moved to Nashville, Tennessee, to attend college, and I continued to let the curing process of the clay that was my life do its work in the furnace. I found a routine and took on a few odd jobs here and there. I won't bore you with the details, but honestly nothing happened for several years. Until one afternoon in 2008 my friend J. T. bought me a donut at Krispy Kreme.

While I was in the beautiful waiting season, I dabbled in live event production. In doing so, my friend J. T. had come to appreciate some of the projects I had worked on. The purpose of the meeting at Krispy Kreme was to see if I could help him with a project he was putting together; he needed some live event production assistance.

He was the manager of a well-known Contemporary Christian rock band that was about to go on tour. He wanted to hire me to design the video content for their show and engineer the equipment to do a triple-wide video wall.

I remember him taking a napkin from the table and sketching out his idea for the set design. The more he sketched, the more excited I got. Here was an opportunity to do something I had begun to enjoy, with a person I had immense respect for. Did I mention he was going to pay me as well? It was an amazing opportunity!

At the end of that meeting, as I licked the sugary glaze off my fingers, he told me to keep the napkin and email an invoice to him so he could put a check with my name on it in the mail.

And then he asked me a question I wasn't expecting: "By the way Luke, what's the name of your company?"

I didn't have an answer. Probably for the first time ever, I didn't have a "brand" name. I wasn't planning on starting a company. Feeling a bit of shame, I told him I would have to get back to him.

I honestly figured that I would tell him to write the check to Luke McElroy, but in the meantime, two other artist managers called me to work on their tours as well.

One thing led to another, and I recognized that God was placing opportunities in my life. Being careful not to control my own destiny, I trusted this was part of the season God had intended in my life, and I may be stepping out from the beautiful wait.

Within a few days, I called up J. T. and shared with him that the name he needed to write on the check was Orange Thread Media.

From the start, I saw Orange Thread as a holding pattern, another element of waiting. I viewed it as something that would prevent me from the long-term commitment of accepting a full-time job at a major company.

It gave me the freedom to start the camp again, once I felt the release from God to move forward.

So I wasn't concerned when, in November of 2011, things started to change at Orange Thread. My first full-time employee was leaving us. And I was excited because he was going to lead a creative team at a very influential church. Almost simultaneously, I received an email from my landlord. Our office was a house just outside of downtown Nashville, and our landlord had sold the building due to financial troubles. While on the phone with our landlord, he proposed to buy me out of my lease if I were to move out within sixty days.

This left me with the realization that my responsibilities as a business owner were quickly evaporating. It may seem to outsiders, that entrepreneurs are free to do what they want. However, most business owners are more tied down in commitments than you may imagine. From staff to building leases, utilities and other long-term commitments, it's not as easy for a business owner to just up and quit.

Couple the disappearance of office space with the sudden change in number of full-time staff and I realized I was free. What I always saw as a holding pattern appeared to begin its initial decent to my final destination. Maybe my time in the oven as clay was about to end and I'd finally leave this season of waiting.

Was this finally God asking me to close the doors of Orange Thread and start building the camp?

I left Nashville for the Christmas holiday and decided to take the first three weeks in January to pray, process, and determine God's plans for the next season of our company. More importantly, I would seek God's plan for the next season of my life.

Those few days in Atlanta after Christmas were life-altering for me. I saw the pause button I hit on the camp idea as a stop button. A new soundtrack was about to start again, and Orange Thread wouldn't be a holding pattern after all.

## Three Questions

Atlanta has always been a safe haven. Aside from being the location of my childhood home, my family, and the church that introduced me to Jesus, Atlanta has become a place of rest and retreat. Absent of that Nashville hustle-hard, never-stop, constant lifestyle, I could focus there.

I remember my first day home was anything but rest and renewal though. I came home to the chaos and never-ending activity of Christmas. My grandfather, my sister, my brother, and his wife were all at the house, eager to participate in the myriad traditions that take place at the McElroy household. Christmas had invaded my plan to find rest and solitude.

Eventually the holiday craze came and went, and I finally found those several days of reflection to seek after what God may have in store for this camp. I assumed that I'd walk away with a clear plan of where and when to start building this camp.

During my time in Atlanta, I asked my dad if I could share some of the details of our company with him, and let him look at some of the direction in which we were headed. I also read a lot of scripture. But most importantly, I spent considerable time on my knees in prayer.

Thinking back, those prayers weren't the familiar "Lord, show me the plans," GPS-like prayers I remember praying on that bus to Panama City Beach. It was obvious that the beautiful waiting season had done something to me. God had cured my clay and done something inside my heart.

I've never heard the audible voice of God. In fact, I don't personally know anyone who has heard His audible voice. Though I don't doubt God could do it, that day in my room I was once again convinced He was speaking to me. What progressed was a conversation where I felt like the Lord asked me three questions. Three questions that changed my life. Forever.

The first question: "Luke, are you a youth minister?" Of course, I wasn't! I hadn't volunteered in a youth ministry since I had moved to Nashville. It wasn't my answer that shocked me as much as the fact that God knew the answer. And that sparked my curiosity.

The second question I felt like He asked was, "Are you planning on gaining influence in the youth ministry world soon?" Again, the answer was a resounding no. I didn't have a plan. I thought God was more about the process than the plan—was I mistaken this whole time?

I didn't have any influence in the world of youth ministry. I knew the youth minister's name at the church I was attending, but he didn't know my name, and I knew enough about him to know he didn't take his students to camp in the summer. But again, God knew this better than I did.

Then the third question. With all that curiosity and all that surprise, I felt like God leaned in and simply whispered, "Then why would I call you to build a youth camp, Luke?"

Wow. I was without words.

No answer was needed to that question. Because I felt the weight of the world lift off my shoulders, and the once Photoshopped picture of that youth camp vanished like vapor. Gone in an instant.

I remember tears began rolling down my cheek. They weren't tears of sadness over something lost, but tears celebrating the clarity I was finally receiving. The joy was followed by a resounding hope that I may be invited back into the process of one day knowing what that picture would entail. And I knew God would reveal each and every detail to me in His perfect timing.

God doesn't ask questions for His benefit. If you don't believe me, go look in scripture for yourself. All throughout the Bible God asks His people questions, not because He is uninformed, but He knows we are uninformed.

Look at Adam and Eve when God was trying to find them in the garden. It wasn't because He had lost them, but more that they were lost themselves. Or Job, when God gave him a shopping list of questions, not to help God understand what was going on in Job's heart, but so that Job would understand what was going on in God's heart.

Even Jesus often answered a question with a question. Therefore, I knew full well that the questions God asked me in those precious days in Atlanta weren't for Him. They were for me.

Around this same time I remember studying the life of Moses. And there's a paramount moment in the early stages of Moses' story, where God asks him a powerful question:

"The Lord said to him, "What is that in your hand?"

"A staff," he replied.

The Lord said, "Throw it on the ground."

So, Moses threw it on the ground and it became a snake, and he ran from it. Then the Lord said to him, "Reach out your hand and take it by the tail." So, Moses reached out and took hold of the snake and it turned back into a staff in his hand.

— Exodus 4:2-5

What's always struck me as interesting in this story is the fact that God chose the staff of Moses. It's not a complex object. It's basically a glorified stick. A stick used to prod and push sheep in a field, giving them direction on where to go.

A staff in Moses' day represented his career and direction. And God was simply asking Moses in this conversation if he would lay it down in front of God. By laying his career and the direction of his life down before God, it became a living creature. Every time Moses picked it back up, it became a dead stick again.

Moses was willing to lay everything he had down before the presence of God. His career, his identity, and ultimately his source of income were placed under the authority of God so that Moses would know where his true source of life came from. Before He ever sent Moses into Egypt, God had to know he was willing to lay his whole life down.

Those three questions became for me a Moses moment, and I started to take the posture that I was ready to lay everything down at the feet of Jesus and see Him take my dead picture and make it come to life.

## CHAPTER THREE

# Coffee to Conference

Moses still doubted the call of God on his life. Even after he had seen his staff turn into a living creature, he doubted. Even after seeing his hand fill with leprosy only to be completely healed by God, he doubted. And if I'm honest with myself, I would have done the exact same thing.

No matter how many miracles Moses may have seen, he wasn't seeing the providential hand of God on his life because he blinded his sight by letting his focus be on his weaknesses, inadequacies, and flaws. Maybe it's because he didn't have the scriptures to remind him that God is always faithful to His promises. Or maybe he was just human, like you and me.

In scripture, we see Moses as quick to remind God of all the inadequacies he embodied. He says to God: "I have never been eloquent, neither in the past nor since you have spoken to me."[2]

Moses knows he can't speak all that well, so how in the world would he be able to convince high-ranking officials in the Egyptian government to let God's chosen people escape slavery (which happens to be the entire working force for the Egyptian regime)?

And once again, God reminds Moses that it's not about the task at hand, but faithfulness and process. God points out to Moses, and all of us, that He is the one who makes our mouths, gives us breath in our lungs, and directs our speech.

## Understanding My Influence

I relate a lot to Moses. Every time God performs a miracle in front of him, he doubts; in fact, after God does two miracles, Moses still questioned God.

The God of the universe, the most creative being to ever exist, just enlightened me that I wasn't called to build a camp. My doubts came not by what was known but what was unknown about the future in that picture.

In hindsight, it was only ever a youth camp because I had convinced myself that it was a youth camp, not because it was a camp. It wasn't necessarily a room full of students for that matter. My own vision clouded my ability to see God's vision. So, like Moses, I said "Yes!" to God once more, and in the waiting, I spent time praying and seeking.

Before I left Atlanta to return to Nashville, I wanted to push a little deeper into what this picture represented. I wanted to ask myself, "Where do I have a little bit of influence?" Since God was putting the concept of my identity and my career on the forefront of my mind, I knew that the industry I was serving and working in might be the key to what God was asking me to pursue. But I couldn't resolve the question.

I had spent most of my recent years working in the live events industry. I was creating visuals for touring artists and people who had incredible influence in culture. But they all *knew their influence*—just looking at some of their social media feeds and the crowds that filled those massive arenas every night convinced me of that.

Then I remembered that statement, "people who didn't fully understand their influence in the world." That was not these touring artists. Was it time for me to enter another period of waiting? Or was I missing it again?

After several days of praying and waiting, God dropped a little glimpse into my life. I did have influence somewhere, influence I hadn't understood myself.

Ever since I had moved to Nashville, I was given several unique opportunities to travel and speak at events, conferences, and churches on the role of creativity in the church, specifically worship services.

What struck me, as I sat in my parent's living room staring out the window into the beautiful blue sky, was that I never did anything to try and gain that influence. (Side note: this is always a key insight to seeing what influence God wants you to use for His kingdom and His purposes.) I didn't have a great blog on the topic. I wasn't the host of a podcast discussing the latest trends in creativity and technology, and I absolutely didn't have any sort of social media following that would justify the mass of people in that picture I saw on the bus to Panama City Beach.

Over time, through the clarity from God, that picture became a bit easier to see. This time I wasn't Photoshopping. It felt more like one of those Magic Eye pictures, where you wait till your eyes can focus beyond the actual texture and see the hidden picture.

The picture wasn't a youth camp. It was a gathering of visual worshippers, technicians, creative art directors, storytellers, and artists who served in the local church. This was more than just an event; it was a community.

This was the beginning of my realizing my own influence, as I was being called into a journey to help others realize their influence. And it didn't come from worldly success or attention. It was simply God saying, "I've got you, Luke."

Those of us in twenty-first century culture confuse the meaning of influence. We associate influence with fame or recognition. And that's simply not the case. The dictionary defines influence as the opportunity to change or affect something or someone. It says nothing about social clout or the number of followers we have on social media. This means that, no matter where we are in life, we all harness the potential to influence culture around us; we just need to open our eyes to the potential.

Our influence in this world is ultimately an extension of the influence God has in our own lives. The more I realize He has influence over every aspect of my calling, my career, my identity, my income and my purpose, the more I realize the potential of the influence I have in my community—influence to help them see their God-influence and free them of worldly bondage.

## Coffee Conversations

Upon returning to Nashville, after a month of what seemed to be a Sabbath of powerful and clarifying con-

NO MATTER WHERE
WE ARE IN LIFE,
WE ALL HARNESS
THE POTENTIAL TO
INFLUENCE CULTURE
AROUND US.

#CREATIVEPOTENTIAL

versations with God, I called a few friends to meet for coffee. I wanted to share some of the visions God had given me and see if they would tell me I was crazy, because I was convinced I needed to make sure that this was God and not some self-concocted plan to gain recognition or fame. The first person I called was Katie.

Let me tell you a little bit about Katie. We first met when a group of us were at the Apple Store, so I knew she had her head on straight because she used Apple computers! Okay, obviously I'm kidding, but she is one of those friends who became fiercely loyal and supportive over the next few months. One of her gifts is being able to share bold truth with honest feedback, but it's never absent of incredible grace and kindness. She has always had a way of telling me that an idea wasn't ready in a way that didn't shame me but empowered me to keep dreaming.

I had also known Katie for several years by then. I trusted that her relationship with God was both authentic and personally intimate. Moreover, Katie had recently started a company to help people get their ideas off the ground. She did so by doing all the "dirty work" in a business. You know, the details, the under-the-surface paperwork like contracts, invoices, emails, calendars, deadlines, project management—I could go on and on. But Katie knew artists well because they were most of her clients. Better yet, she had been involved with several conferences and live events that had specifically worked to gather artists together.

There was no doubt she would be eager to hear the next chapter in the story, because like many close friends of mine, she knew the camp idea well. She tells many people about one of the first real conversations we had, and how it was dominated by the idea of how I was going to start a camp.

I believed wholeheartedly that she cared about seeing me find my purpose more than she cared about my being successful from a worldly point of view, which made her the perfect person to share this idea with.

We sat down at our neighborhood Starbucks, a place we had met numerous times before to share updates on each other's lives. As we caught up, sharing Christmas stories and the drama of her having to clean out her mother's hoarder-like basement, I eventually shared the update on all God had done in my heart during my time in Atlanta.

I remember saying these words: "Katie, I don't think I'm supposed to build a youth camp." And as her surprise turned to excitement that God was up to something in my life, she leaned in to hear the rest of the story with eager expectation. I asked her, "Do you think I am crazy to start planning a conference that would become a gathering place for a creative community of artists, engineers, and storytellers in the church?"

She quickly replied, "No," and after a brief pause, as if she was allowing herself to assess the power of the words that would follow, she looked up and continued, "In fact, you have to do this, Luke!"

I don't know why, but I wasn't convinced. Was she just saying this to make me feel better about not building a camp whose potential had so engrossed me? I wanted to make sure she thought this was something *I had to do.* So I asked again, "Are you sure about that? I mean, I don't have any social media following. I don't own a magazine, a radio program, a podcast, or any sort of platform to get the word out. I'm not a conference guy! Right?"

With a bit of a smile, as if she knew something I didn't, she said "Yup! And that's exactly why you have to do this."

She was right, but I still had my doubts, just like Moses with the leprous hand. So to test her own conviction to this idea, I asked something that would cause her to have skin in the game too.

"Katie, if you really think I am supposed to do this, then why don't you help me plan the first conference?"

To my surprise, she said, "Okay! Let me know when you want to get started."

## Dream Again

It's one thing when you feel like your calling has been confirmed. It's an entirely different thing when you know that God is confirming your calling through the people who know Him and walk with you the most. When a friend, who knows your story, not only affirms but jumps into the pit with you to help you along your journey, it's confirmation that represents the picture of God's whole body unified to accomplish His great commission.

Unbeknownst to Katie, I needed to talk with another friend about what God was telling me. So I called my friend Nick.

Let me start by saying that Nick is one of the smartest people I have ever met. I'm not talking about the ability to take written tests or fill out multiple choice questions well to score a 100 percent on a final exam. No, I'm talking about the type of intelligence that learned how to code Unix in a few days, was the first one who told me about 3-D printers, and the type of guy who could reverse engineer almost any form of technology he touched.

I didn't call Nick solely because of his IQ level either. We became friends because he used to work for a youth camp, and when I mentioned on our first interaction that I "was going to build a camp one day," we immediately became best friends.

More than any of his worldly genius, I knew he had a passion to be part of kingdom-minded activity. He wanted his work to matter, and I knew he would give me a very honest and level-headed response to this somewhat crazy idea of going from a camp to a conference.

In what felt like déjà vu, my conversation with Nick was nearly identical to my conversation with Katie. Not only did he say, "You *are* the one to start that conference," it was as if he had just been waiting for me to tell him this idea. Have you ever experienced a moment like that? You're telling a story and the other person introduces a confident smile, as if to say, "I've been waiting for you to say this, Luke." And with that smile came another confirmation.

Nick's confirmation also came with an acceptance to be involved in launching this God idea, and before I knew it, there were three of us on the team.

Within just a few days, I had two of my closest, smartest friends in the pit with me. And I started to dream again. The difference was the dreaming seemed God-ordained and God-approved, and I had two other people who were convinced as much as I was that we had to do this.

Never in my life have I had one of those moments when I looked at the project that lay before me and spoke these words over my life: "I can't *not* do this." I know that's a double negative, but if I were to move on with my life and not take a bold step of faith, I'd regret it for the rest of my life! And with that, we forged ahead, trusting and following every step God led us to take.

CHAPTER FOUR

# The Name at 2:00 A.M.

The first time I recall having a boss was in the spring of 1996. It wasn't really a boss because I was just volunteering. It was also the first time I can remember doing anything technical for the local church. His name was Tim Honsalek, but I called him Mr. H. His last name was a lot to process as a kid.

What made this story so memorable was because Mr. H believed in me and encouraged me to serve regardless of my shortcomings or weaknesses. I was diagnosed with ADHD (attention deficit hyperactivity disorder) at a young age, which meant I often had a tough time focusing as a child. But Mr. H never worried that I wouldn't do a great job, and because he believed in me, I think it empowered me to put my all into that job.

The job wasn't all that difficult, but it did require an attention to detail. I was running the lights for a church musical. This was before the church had a lighting console that allowed you to program cues and hit the next button when you wanted the next "scene" to appear. Instead, you took the overall intensity down, reset your individual lights on faders to the right, and then when ready returned the grand master (the slider that controlled all the lights' brightness) to its original, full position.

Wanting to do a great job, I set a look, ran over to Mr. H, and asked if he liked it. He pretty much always did because he believed in me. So I'd run back, write down the numbers, and return to get his approval for the next scene. This continued for the duration of one early rehearsal.

For some reason, my experience with Mr. H seems to resemble the process I am inclined to have whenever I'm working in my God calling, and it gets me in trouble. I don't think God wants me to go *do* something and then run back to Him to get a blessing and move on. That exact mindset is what got me so far from the original picture God had given me in the first place. And I wasn't going to do that again.

What may have been okay as a child wasn't going to be okay with God and this conference. Because there's a big difference between a childlike faith and a childish faith. Childish faith is trying to do everything without God and ask Him to bless it, when a childlike faith wants to do everything with God and He will naturally bless the things He's involved in.

Trying to control my own story is what pushed me far from God's intent for my life, and I didn't want to run that same road again. Therefore, at every planning meeting we had about the conference, we made sure to ask God to lead, rather than asking God to bless the things we were doing. I know it's subtle, but for us it helped us keep a healthy perspective on our role in God's story.

This wasn't our vision. We were merely stewards of God's vision.

When God calls you to something that is of His will and in line with His purposes for your life, He wants your faithfulness to become a conduit for *Him* to do the work. It's the way we can know that He is in the details of the things we're working on; God is seemingly working all the details on your behalf. It's biblical. It's not God's nature to be disconnected from His purpose.

There's nothing inherently wrong in asking for God's blessing. Having God's blessing is a holy and reverent prayer. But for me, I wanted to have more of a Psalm 90 approach: "Let the favor of the Lord our God be upon us, and establish the work of our hands."[3]

In my life, every time I've had to ask for a blessing from God, it's been proof that I've been trying to control the outcome of whatever I'm wanting. That could be a job opportunity, a business idea, a relationship, or even the blessing to leave or quit something. One afternoon, I had this thought about God's blessing: "Is asking God to bless something another way I am trying to control God again?"

There it is—that nagging pride that wells up every time I start something. It's destructive because it makes me think I am capable enough to do something without God. What an appalling thought! And it hit me: if I am truly within the will of God, won't He naturally bless whatever I'm working on because it's His vision and His intent in the first place?

Where I used to pray something like "Lord, will you bless the work I've done here?" I try to exchange with,

"Lord, will you guide my work to be in step with your purpose?"

I want to always be working *with* God, not merely *for* God, because there seems to always be an intimacy in the "with" that has always been absent for me in the "for." I think this is what God wanted out of Moses too, as I've come to process his life and God's purposes.

There's a phrase in scripture that is repeated a few times in Moses' story that has always stood out to me. It's the phrase "the Lord burned with anger." That's a pretty intense thought if you try to wrap your head around it. I never want my name and that statement ever to come across God's mind.

It appears numerous times in scripture, but mostly when God is trying to tell Moses that He's fed up with the Israelites as Moses is leading them out of Egypt into the Promised Land. Moses isn't just asking God to bless the things he is involved in, as if God isn't taking part in the process too. You'll notice that even Moses understood this key principle of being involved in God's original intent.

Look at what Moses tells God after one of these "burning with anger" moments in Numbers 14:13-16.

> Moses said to the Lord, "Then the Egyptians will hear about it! By your power you brought these people up from among them. And they will tell the inhabitants of this land about it. They have already heard that you, O Lord, are with these people and that you, O Lord, have

been seen face to face, that your cloud stays over them, and that you go before them in a pillar of cloud by day and a pillar of fire by night. If you put all these people to death, leaving none alive, the nations who have heard this report about you will say, 'The Lord was not able to bring these people into the land he promised them on oath, so he slaughtered them in the wilderness.'"

Here's a man so in step with the activity and intimacy of God that he can say bold and powerful words to the Creator of the universe. I'm inspired by the partnership he and God had in his time here on earth. It wasn't that Moses wanted God to spare the Israelites so that Moses' reputation would be noticed by others. Moses wanted God to spare the Israelites for God's reputation and to further God's purposes in the world.

God always invites me into something that He purposed to begin with. But in my desire to make something of myself, I try to invite God into the things I've tried to purpose. I had it all backwards with the camp. I believe, wholeheartedly, one of the reasons Katie, Nick, and I felt so aligned with the purposes of God so quickly in our process was because we never asked God to "bless" what we were doing; we asked God to "involve us" in what He was doing.

## And Then There Were Four

As amazing as Nick and Katie are at what they do, something was missing. As we prayed to be involved in

God's plans, we felt like that missing something was one more person. So I was always alert whenever I would meet someone, eager to know if they were the person God intended to complete our team. It's amazing how the seemingly random events in your life seem to become supernaturally ordained when you're hyperaware of God's presence in your life.

One afternoon I found myself playing Cornhole at a friend's house. Since you need a partner to play, I began asking around to find a partner interested in playing with me. One guy said, "Sure!" He introduced himself as JoeAngel, and even though we lost the game, we gained a friendship.

We lost touch a bit after the Cornhole game, but after a few months, a tour reunited the two of us. After boarding the bus for the first night, I threw my bag in the back and walked back toward the front of the bus. Lo and behold, there was JoeAngel. This tour was how we became close friends and how the conversation of the conference eventually came up. It was so obvious as I spent time with him that God had ordained the two of us to meet and that he would become the missing element of our core team.

JoeAngel also had a rich history in the youth ministry sphere growing up, as a key student leader at Acquire the Fire (ATF). It wasn't his time at ATF that made him a good fit for the team, but rather his love for people, his vast array of relationships, and his desire to help creative-minded individuals that made him connect with our team and join our mission as we ran with fervency toward this vision.

The first time I told him about the vision for the conference, he lit up like a Christmas tree. Unlike a lot in our generation who are looking to climb a ladder, JoeAngel was different; that was nowhere near his desire. He already had that. He had worked with some of the most recognizable names in the worship and Contemporary Christian community, so this was more likely to slow him down than help him grow. This is why he fit our team so well, because he was willing to leverage all his love and heart for God to impact and invest in a community of people who didn't quite know the potential they had.

I remember saying to him in my office one afternoon, "JoeAngel, you know we'll never make money off this idea, right? I mean, no one is getting paid and this is going to cost a fortune."

Without missing a beat, JoeAngel responded, "I never said anything about money. Why do you think that matters to me?"

I thought to myself, *So he must be rich.* Okay, I'm only partially kidding about the rich part, but his response about not being focused on money was 100 percent genuine, and I invited JoeAngel to the next team meeting to introduce him to Katie and Nick.

What was three became four, and together we continued to regularly meet, pray, and plan. Over the course of several months of planning, we found ourselves preparing and writing our details for a conference that remained nameless.

It was only a matter of time before God would give us the name that would become so much more than a name to this community, but a picture that would shift our thinking to the role creativity, technology, and art play in the realm of worship and church.

That name would soon come at 2:00 a.m.

## If You Say So

Every movement needs a name and every name needs a meaning.

I wish I knew that back in 2012 when the word "SALT" came to me for the first time. It's one of those words we hear so often that we rarely stop to think about what it means in a different context.

I also wish I had a better story for where the name came from. But I don't.

People have asked me over the years if SALT is an acronym, and some have even assumed one. The best one I've heard on the acronym side is that it stands for "Sound and Light Team." I can only laugh hysterically at some of these ideas because it's such a reminder of why we need more creativity in the church than some cute-sounding acronym. (I hope you don't have an acronym for your church's creative arts ministry, or that would be awkward right about now.)

Others have asked if it represents a specific scripture; the answer is no. It has no reference to Elisha or the covenant of salt from the Old Testament. It's not from one of the Gospels either, even though all have come to support the name. Let me tell you where the name came from.

I had recently done an event with Israel Houghton, and he had likely sung his entire catalog of hits. But for some reason there was one song I couldn't get out of my head. "Let the redeemed of the Lord say so, let the redeemed of the Lord say so, say so, say so."

If you've heard this song before, you're probably now humming it to yourself as I was, over and over. (If you haven't heard the song and want it stuck in your head, feel free to search "Say So" on Spotify or YouTube right now.)

Does that ever happen to you? You sing a song so often that it comes back to haunt you at the worst times? For me, it was at two o'clock in the morning and I wanted to be sleeping. But instead "Say So" was on repeat in my head. And it kept me awake.

The bridge of that song repeats the phrase "to be salt and light in the world, in the world." It's probably sung five or six times, but over the course of the event, it's likely that we sang it countless times.

When those words haunted me in the middle of that night, it hit me. This community was to be named SALT. And what does salt do? It flavors. It heals. It preserves. And it causes people to thirst.

It was the perfect name for a community who used technology, creativity, arts, media, story, and design to help people experience the presence of God. It was short, simple, and memorable. But it was also a mini parable, a story if you will, that would allow us to remember the role it plays.

And there it was. A name. A picture. A story. Something that invited people in and sent them out with purpose. For we, as the creative community in the world, are called to be the SALT in the world. Creativity would become salt in our culture by flavoring the gospel message, healing those hurt by the church, preserving the story of God, and causing people to thirst for Jesus in a world desperately in need.

## CHAPTER FIVE

# And Then Another Wall

There we were, meeting regularly, leaning into all that God had in store for this gathering that would one day come to fruition. And we had a name. These two things gave us significant momentum. Within a few weeks, we had a schedule, and I was starting to meet with a few friends to see if we could find a home for the recently imagined SALT Conference.

Before I continue into the chaos that ensued in these early days, I need to tell you about Joe. Joe, not to be confused with JoeAngel who is on our team, was my creative pastor at the church I was attending. Since this vision wasn't birthed out of a church specifically, we wanted to make sure that we had some amazing church leaders and pastors become metaphorical "elders" on a leadership team.

Joe was member number one of that unnamed, informal board. Having worked at my church for well over a decade, I knew that Joe had a loyalty to the bride of Christ and the body of the local church like few I have encountered. He had roots. But furthermore, he was doing some incredibly creative things.

One time he built a literal altar in the middle of the room, with fake blood and what seemed to be a burnt lamb, for a series our church was going through that referenced the Levitical sacrifices. The team he had assembled had also created some very beautiful videos and short stories, along with a set design that was always very organic and highly engaging, all while maintaining a margin in ministry I have envied for some time.

I knew Joe would be a phenomenal resource to this conference and to this community. So we got lunch and started dreaming. It was a long lunch to say the least because he was immediately on board and conjuring up ways we could maximize the impact this gathering could have on people like him who served in churches around the country.

Upon arriving back to the church, Joe shared that he thought our church would be a good fit for the conference. Decent in its size to support the workshops and community groups we wanted to implement, but not too large to swallow people up in a massive worship center. It was perfect. And with that news, our team started planning.

Our progress continued at a hurried pace. Our team did several site visits at the church so we could orchestrate all the tiny details that consume a conference. We met with Joe along with the rest of the worship and arts team to discuss production needs, the role of their staff, etc. All the while, Joe was working his magic behind the scenes with the staff in various ministry teams to ensure that everyone knew what was happening and we'd be able to get approval to block the rooms we needed for the duration that was required to pull this off.

## The Final Meeting

A lot took place in a relatively short amount of time as Joe was working on details at the church, while our team went to work on confirming speakers, designing logos, building out a website, and finalizing our ticket price. Piece by piece, the conference began to take shape. What originated as a vague concept months prior was now much clearer. We were almost ready to announce the conference!

The joy on our team was almost overwhelming. Everyone was in a rhythm. Everything was falling into place in near perfect timing. Our team was ready to make our big announcement to the world. So I called Joe and decided to set up one final meeting with him and the church.

It was October 4, 2012. And my goal was to put together a simple agreement to make sure our team and the church were on the same page. This contract would also become a tangible representation of a home for this community, the last piece needed to finish the puzzle. Once that piece was in place, we could share the exciting news that our core team, keynotes, and many involved in production had been harboring for the past few months.

This was a big meeting for me, so I wanted to get there early and be well prepared. When I got there, no one was in the worship center. So I grabbed a seat on the steps of the stage and waited.

We had met there every time before, and since I was early, I just waited for the others to show up. As I waited, I looked down at the time. It was 12:45 now and the meeting was at 12:30. Something didn't feel right, so I called Joe.

Joe picked up and said, "Hey Luke! Have you met with Bob?" Joe was home with two sick children. He apologized for not being there, but assured me that Bob would take care of me.

I had not met Bob in any of our previous meetings, which is why Bob assumed the meeting would be in Joe's office, not the worship center. In my attempt to be early, I was now fifteen minutes late to the most important meeting in our team's journey. So I ran across the parking lot to the church offices.

Upon arriving at his office, I found Bob. Just Bob.

I extended my hand. "Hey, I'm—"

Before I could finish, Bob interrupted, not to introduce himself but to say, "We can't host your conference."

I was shell-shocked. I didn't say a word. Part of me was livid because I hadn't even had a chance to introduce myself, let alone share the vision that we felt God had instilled in our hearts. He just went straight to a no. It felt violating, if I were honest.

I couldn't process the words that had just come out of Bob's mouth. I don't remember exactly what came after he realized I wasn't talking. It was like everything else became silent as I let those words sink in. Then I realized he was talking again.

"We just can't change all these classes and Bible studies, because it will cause too much of a displacement of people. Furthermore, I haven't been told by senior leadership that I am supposed to move all these classes, so it's just not going to happen guys."

I'm so glad Bob had Joe on speakerphone at that moment. Because Joe stepped in at the exact moment Bob finished. I probably wouldn't have been ready to talk anyway. I was still processing all that had just happened in the last few seconds. Then it hit me.

Here I am, this time with a team around me, in another starting gate. This one we were convinced was *God's starting gate*. Stuck. Again!

How had this happened? Had I missed the picture of what God was calling us to do again? Was I once more out of line with the purpose God had for our team? How was it that we had journeyed this far in this process, only to get another stuck starting gate?

Frustration subdued to the swelling of sadness. That's when I recognized it wasn't the same feeling I had when I first tried to pry the starting gates open. This was a much different feeling. It's as if the announcer was getting ready to fire off his gun to start the race, but before he did, he said, "Are you ready? Get set ... " and never said the word go.

The only thing worse than hearing Bob say no to me was the reality that I faced: I still had to tell the team.

All my life, I grew up convinced that God had one thing in store for me. Then He tells me that the one thing I thought was for me wasn't for me after all and He had a new thing. And now, I'm being told by Bob that this new thing, which I knew was from God, wasn't for me either. I have to tell my team that we are back to square one. No host church. No home. And I must do that while trying to lead as well. But I felt defeated. I was bummed, and to be honest, angry at God.

After composing my thoughts, it was time to face the fear and share with the team all that had taken place. We weren't going to have a conference that upcoming February.

Then came the leadership lesson. How do I walk a team through another wall while still believing wholeheartedly that we were operating in the will of God? I had to learn how to know that the wall before us wasn't there to stop us but to remind us that our journey is about intimacy with Him, rather than doing something for Him.

I told our team it was time for us to take a break. We would stop planning and working, and instead focus our time on just being with God again in prayer. We had to know for sure if the still small voice of God was still saying "go" or if this was us trying to Photoshop another picture into being.

As we stopped, we pursued God in the waiting. We trusted that this wall before us wasn't a sign to quit, but to press in and watch God use it for His glory in His timing. But I must tell you, this was not an easy season to endure. As a leader, I felt immense failure. As a disciple, I felt intense loneliness. And as a man, I felt like I let friends down.

## Seemingly Impossible

There's a story in Genesis that is astounding. It's about Abraham, the one whom God had chosen to give a family so great that neither the stars in the sky nor the sands in the ocean could accurately account for the number of his eventual descendants. And yet, at a very old age, Abraham's wife, Sarah, gave birth to a son. This was all that Abraham wanted. A son from his beautiful wife.

And God, after years of making Abraham wait, finally gifted him with Isaac.

But then, only a page turn from the birth of Isaac, God asks something almost unthinkable from Abraham. God asks him to take his son Isaac—the one whom he longed for his entire life and loved beyond everything else in his universe—up to the mountain to sacrifice him. Can you think about that for a second?

If you have children, could you fathom this request from God? A request that would require you to give up the thing you love in life more than anything else to show God that He still reigns supreme in your life and deserves the sacrifice?

And surprisingly, Abraham goes through with God's request. Genesis 22 shares the account of this story and tells us that the two of them began to hike up the mountain to give a sacrifice to their Lord. Isaac was skeptical because they didn't have a lamb to slaughter.

But he trusted his father, and Abraham trusted the Father. And we read this:

> "When they reached the place God had told him about, Abraham built an altar there and arranged the wood on it. He bound his son Isaac and laid him on the altar, on top of the wood. Then he reached out his hand and took the knife to slay his son. But the angel of the Lord called out to him from heaven, 'Abraham! Abraham!'
> 'Here I am,' he replied.
> 'Do not lay a hand on the boy,' he said. 'Do not do anything to him. Now I know that you

fear God, because you have not withheld from
me your son, your only son.'"[4]

Sometimes God's plans don't make sense to us. And
in this moment, He wanted to know that Abraham loved
and feared God more than everything else in the world.
And of course, the gracious, loving, merciful God didn't
let Isaac die on that altar either, but it did cause pause
for both to recognize the role and position that God had
in each of their lives.

To be willing to sacrifice your own son is seemingly
impossible. And I'm not going to say that I loved the SALT
Conference we had been planning like a parent would love
their first-born child, but this story spoke to me in that
season. I had to recognize that my love for God had to be
greater than my love for anything else. For Abraham, it
was his son. For me and our team, it was this gathering.

God wanted to see where our true love resided. Was
our team willing to lay down the conference to know for
ourselves and for God that He was our ultimate love and
affection?

For us, this wasn't just another wall but a bit of a trial.
We didn't see the setback in the venue as Satan trying
to destroy our hope as much as we saw it as God saying
to the angels and probably Satan, "Watch this, I'll show
you that they don't love their call more than the one who
called them into it."

I've tried to think about what might have taken place
after that awkward encounter with Abraham and Isaac
on that mountain. Think about it. Isaac now believes that
his father was possibly going to go through with the act

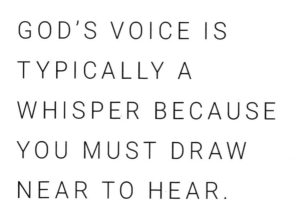

GOD'S VOICE IS
TYPICALLY A
WHISPER BECAUSE
YOU MUST DRAW
NEAR TO HEAR.

#CREATIVEPOTENTIAL

of sacrificing him on that altar. Though he didn't, I'd think the walk down that mountain would be a very awkward conversation.

In my imagination, I can see the two of them walking down the path back to the valley where they lived. On one side, the intimacy between them had been robbed because Isaac was almost killed by the hand of his father. On the other side, there was an amazing increase in intimacy that arose between the two of them along with God because God was faithful in His promise.

That's a bit how our team felt in those next few months. There was a part of us that felt like our relationships with one another had been robbed by this guy named Bob at the church. But we also walked with a new form of intimacy as we drew closer to God to understand the whispers of His next words.

I've learned in my short time here on earth that God gets the glory when we lean in. It's probably why He whispers too. I don't think He whispers to make it tough for us to hear Him or to cause strain in our life. I think God's voice is typically a whisper because you must draw near to hear. What a beautiful picture of a God who is relentlessly in love with His children, that He lowers his voice to invite more of you into His presence.

## Freefall from Heaven

After a few months had passed, I went back to Atlanta for Christmas with my family, and our team spread out across the country as they went back to their own friends and family for the holiday season. We hadn't had a formal meeting together since the dreadful meeting that took place in October, but I can say with certainty that I was praying a very consistent prayer: "God, if this really is you, then you're going to have to drop a venue into my lap from seemingly nowhere!"

I tried to reason with God while I was in Atlanta by saying things like, "I've looked at this place and it won't work. I don't know the pastor of the church down here, but you could have him call me! You know my number."

To be transparent, I had no clue what I was praying, but I knew that I was in this because God had led us here, and we were so eagerly listening that I was serious when I asked him over and over to drop a venue in our laps. I was trying to get close to hear His whisper.

By the time I had arrived back in Nashville from the Christmas and New Year holidays, I had somewhat transitioned my progress on the SALT Conference from probability to the beautiful wait again. I had almost resigned to return to a period of waiting, like Nehemiah did, for God to open some doors.

Luckily I didn't have to wait as long as Nehemiah. One early morning in January I walked into a coffee shop just around the corner from my office, a place I had been to countless times before. A friend was sitting at a table, so I went up to him to say hello. And he was sitting with a gentleman I did not recognize.

"Luke, I want you to meet Charlie," my friend Mike said. "I was just telling him about the conference you guys have coming up soon on creativity, and he was really eager to know a bit more about what it's all about."

Inside me, the tension of a failed past and the robbed intimacy began to swell up. My blood pressure rose, probably because that statement was a bit of a stressful reminder that I still didn't have it all figured out. There's a wealth of shame in a statement like that and I couldn't help but wonder if this would be the ghost that would follow me forever. Would we be the team that failed forever? Would I always be known as the guy who could never get a conference off the ground?

The fear became near paralyzing because I didn't know this man, and I'd have to face the facts with strangers, as this would be the way I'd be introduced to them. So I tried with everything in me to explain the situation without going into too much detail, and let Charlie know that we weren't going to be having a conference anymore.

"Well, God closed some doors, and we're back in a waiting period for Him to help us identify what the next step is for our team. We really need a host church at this point, or that may not happen anytime soon," I said.

And then Charlie spoke up. "Well, Luke, I'd love to have you come to my office sometime. Our church may be a perfect fit."

I was somewhat dumbfounded. Did Charlie not know what I just said? It was as if he was completely ignoring that this wasn't going to happen, and he was dropping his name in as a possible host. As you can imagine, I eagerly set up a meeting.

That meeting was the first time I had ever stepped into Charlie's church. And there I was, meeting with Charlie. The nameplate on his desk read "Associate Pastor." His church is in the heart of an area called Music Row—a place in Nashville where much of the music industry has its roots.

It was there that I realized God may have answered our prayer after all. Maybe he was dropping a venue into our lap! In a highly creative neighborhood, with a church who had a vision of being part of the creative fabric of our culture. One who had deep roots in serving, loving, shepherding, and discipling so many creative leaders in its long history as a church. Maybe SALT wasn't supposed to get its start in a suburban church but more in this urban environment in the center of the rich artistic heritage and creative tradition that had made Nashville so recognizable to the world.

When Charlie turned to me and said, "Let's do this, Luke!" It was so different from before. He was the leadership team. He was the decision maker. There wasn't anyone else who could step in and say no. This is how beautiful God's plan is. He provides when it's His plan.

It's not the story I would have chosen for our team. But I believe it's a better story than we could have ever written ourselves. So often I just want to have it all work when God gives us the green light. But God doesn't get the glory in our concocted plans. He gets the glory when we're put in a position where we can't do something by our own strength, and it still comes to fruition.

When our team had come to the place where we couldn't do a single thing on our own to make this God-calling a reality, God stepped in and provided a way. It's as if God orchestrated all of this to remind us to operate in light of His calling, not our own abilities.

I know it feels like a bow at the end of the story, but I promise it was far from easy from this point on.

Nonetheless, the starting gate wasn't stuck anymore, and we were off and running.

There were a few things that I remember being a major challenge. For one, the church had no tables or chairs. And we wanted to serve a dinner for everyone at the same time. We didn't have a penny to spend either. So we called everyone we knew who had a ton of tables and chairs. With about three weeks to spare, we found someone to donate every single chair (almost three hundred) and all the tables for dinner.

Next was parking. We were expecting somewhere between two hundred and three hundred people at the conference, but there was only parking for a hundred. This wasn't something we could control. I wish I could say that we had a business miraculously donate the additional hundred spots, but it never came through. It was a hassle. It wasn't pretty, and it was far from ideal.

Then came the production. For months, Nick and his team tried to come up with ideas. But this new church was different from the original one we had been talking with. At the first church we could have hung stuff from the ceilings, projected on the side walls, and created the atmosphere we wanted. But this new church had windows without curtains, nowhere in the ceiling to hang anything, and a much smaller stage that couldn't entirely be cleared off.

I remember Nick telling me when we were two and a half weeks out that he didn't have a single clue about what to do with the set design. That wouldn't come until thirteen days before load-in day. And with thirteen days out, Nick felt like God gave him the idea for our first year's set. And that set was amazing. But it took a heck of a lot of work.

Then there was the fire department incident. About an hour before registration began, our team was programming lighting and video cues in the main session. The amount of haze we were using in the main room set off the fire alarm, which caused three fire trucks and a handful of police officers to engulf the streets in front of the church. Can you imagine what it must have been like to be outside waiting to register for a conference while an army of fire trucks and police cars come blaring up, causing the officers and firefighters to run through the front door? This is a moment that our team laughs about to this day!

Just because we felt the wind of heaven propelling us toward the launch of the first SALT Conference didn't mean it would be easy. The two things I realized I needed more than ever were perseverance and resiliency. Stepping into your calling means you are stepping into battle. Because when God's people are in the sweet spot of their purpose, the enemy will do whatever he can to throw you off course. Heaven is behind you, the cross had the final word, and the Spirit is with you in battle as you persevere through the process.

When I know that I'm running the race I'm destined to be running, I've learned to run with the confidence of the cross behind me. It's never my goal to just cross the finish line. I want my resilience to allow me to cross that finish line with nothing left for another race. We only get one life on this earth, so run in a way that leaves nothing for the next life.

## Recognizing Faithfulness

With mere minutes remaining before registration began, I stood with those men and women who had walked this journey with me. Our core team, the keynote speakers, our lead volunteer coordinators, my full-time staff at Orange Thread, and my parents were all in the room together. Tears ran down my face as I wept before them and before God. I recognized the faithfulness of God and what it feels like to step into the creative potential that had been predestined for me and see the fruit of my God-given calling.

All this while, I had begun to think that God was taking me on this journey to create something for others. Something to help them recognize their influence in the world. Standing there in that moment, we all recognized that God was writing a story for His glory and we were characters in that story.

It caused me to realize the influence God wants so desperately in my own life. Our divine creative potential will only exist when we step into the fullness of who we are in Christ—hidden within His glorious presence.

God's not here to play games. He loves His lost and hurting children so much that He will do nearly anything to reach them. Even if it means nonexistent youth camps, Krispy Kreme napkins, and turned-down conference venues. This process had grown my faith exponentially, and I was much closer to God. Maybe that is exactly what the process of discovering your creative potential is after all.

Even as I sit here today, having written this story for you, I recognize something very powerful. That picture

God gave to me on that Skittle-covered seat on my way to Panama City Beach wasn't a picture of what the end of my calling would look like. That picture was only the beginning.

# INTERMISSION

What you finished reading wasn't just my story or my team's story. I believe it's all *our* story. Your story may not be exact, but God is calling you into something, and He is obsessed with the process not the product. He will do anything to make sure that your story is more for the one who calls you than the call itself.

Maybe you see yourself in my story as you process what God has in store for your own calling. Or maybe part of our team's journey has brought clarity about something in your own journey, I don't know. But I believe God to be a God who deserves all the credit.

I've called this chapter the intermission, which is a bit weird for a book, I know. It's vital though. Because I need you to take a brief pause before you start the next act. Go grab popcorn or your favorite candy. If you're reading this on a plane, maybe ask the flight attendant for a Coke.

Regardless of where you are, I want you to take a breath.

I want you to take a breath because of how I've structured this book. The first act was one story we all find ourselves in as we identify our calling. The act that lies before you are principles I believe will help anyone unleash their God-given potential.

Act II isn't as linear as Act I was. Therefore, I want you to take a breath and reflect for a few minutes. Maybe put the book down and pick it back up in a day. It's okay, you'll be able to pick it right back up.

## What Happened Next

February 7, 2012. A day that's still on my calendar as I look back.

It's the day that Nick, Katie, and I first met at that coffee shop to begin dreaming together about what this new vision of a conference would look like. We didn't realize that it was our first meeting. The calendar entry simply says "Coffee with Nick and Katie."

Little did we know that was the first time God began to deposit bits and pieces of what soon became SALT.

One coffee gathering turned into many more, and we talked about a variety of ideas, spent a considerable time praying for this conference as well as for each other, and we read scripture. I wouldn't say it was a Bible study by any means, but it felt more like a Bible study than a strategy session.

I remember Katie telling me several weeks after these meetings started that she never put notes into her Evernote notebooks because she didn't think this was a real conference. Not that she didn't believe what we were planning was good, but we were more concerned about sharing what God was writing on our hearts, than writing down ideas for us to execute later.

That was a pivotal point for our team. We realized that more than just schedules, speaker ideas, themes, logos, and set designs, God was instilling inside us a series of principles and beliefs that would become the manifesto for our gatherings.

We scoured scripture to affirm these deposited words. We wrestled together with what it meant to truly be SALT as creatives. We looked at the role of creativity in the Sunday corporate expression of worship, and we questioned every single element of a contemporary church service.

For our team, this was a season where God was pouring His plans, His purposes, and His promises into our beings. Not so we'd *do* right away but so that we would be filled with the presence and desires of God. We may have seen it as waiting, but I wonder if the waiting was so God could fill up our lives with His purposes and presence, and we would be able to create out of the overflow of His creative potential?

As He poured in, we realized that the things He was teaching us in these days were the principles that would lay a foundation for this conference and ultimately this community.

## The Next Act Begins

As the days unfolded between February 7, 2012, and the moment we gathered in that chapel for the last time as a team before the start of SALT13 (on October 21, 2013), a lot of processing went into how someone reaches their creative potential. What I believe God gave us was meant for more than just for those who run the creative and technical elements in the church; it was meant for a broader audience, which is why this book now exists.

These principles aren't only for those who have attended one of our gatherings. Until this book, SALT was the only vehicle God had given our team to teach and equip others through these principles. But I can ensure you that they are applicable to everyone as you decipher for yourself what it is that God may be calling you to for your life.

In Act II, I'll walk you through what I believe are the four principles of maximizing your potential.

For every principle, there are two chapters. One is to help us understand the principle itself, pouring a foundation on the *why* as we explore our own application. Following that is a chapter that functions as a practical guide, giving you the *what* behind each principle as well. I've structured it this way so that you may sense the pouring in that God provided us in those early meetings as a team. And as you sense God pouring into your own life, you'll see the joy, beauty, and influence you have in this world.

We start with the principle of **unique**. At our core, God has made every human being unique, and it's imperative to recognize that your calling isn't going to be like another's. From there we'll explore what it means to be the best version of your unique self by exploring **excellence**. Then I'll introduce **collaboration** where we can see what it means to let iron sharpen iron and recognize that we're called to excellent uniqueness in the context of a community. Lastly I'll help you see where transformation takes place when the best unique community engages in the **contagiousness** of God's story and lives are forever impacted for eternity.

Wrapping up, the last two chapters of the book will leave you with a few final thoughts on specific limiters of your potential.

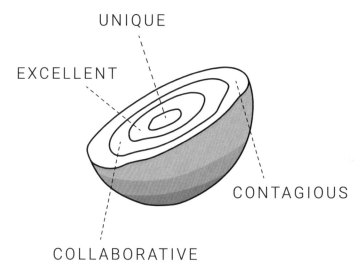

The best way to think about these principles is to imagine one of those candy Gobstoppers® (also known as jawbreakers to some). A Gobstopper is comprised of numerous layers of sugar, each a different color. If you were to cut one of these rock-hard candies in half, you would see several layers of colors on top of each other, with a core in the middle.

I eagerly pray that the pages to follow are nothing short of transformative. I pray that you're able to absorb the principles, process, and purposes that lay before you. I pray that you will see yourself as a creative, life-changed Gobstopper. So go ahead, put the book down for a minute, take a short break, and when you come back, we'll begin Act II.

# ACT II

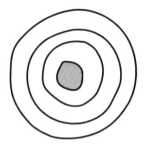

## CHAPTER SEVEN

# Unique: Recognizing Our Value

Have you ever seen the show *Shark Tank?*

If not, it's a show where hopeful entrepreneurs pitch ideas to wealthy "sharks," or financial investors, with the goal of walking out with a certain amount of money to launch, grow, or save a business. It's a powerful example of the value of uniqueness in our culture.

If an entrepreneur pitches an idea that one of the sharks has seen or heard in the past, the shark immediately loses interest in the rest of the pitch. But if it's an idea that seems original, something they can see becoming successful, they will put an offer on the table and invest.

Often Kevin O'Leary, one of the sharks, will ask if the entrepreneur has a patent. If not a patent, he wants to know if the idea or design is proprietary, because O'Leary knows that patents offer a form of protection around a process, product, or idea. A patent is almost like a certification of uniqueness. With it comes immense value and increased revenue potential in marketplace, thus increasing the interest level for O'Leary.

The sharks are just one example of how our culture values uniqueness. The more unique something is, the more you and I will pay for it. We marvel at custom-built houses and pay a premium to live in them. We discount the tract or spec houses that pop up by the dozen when a new development is unearthed near our home. Men will spend thousands on a custom-tailored suit at a high-end store when they could pay a mere $80 for a basic suit at Walmart.

Custom is unique. Unique is valuable. The rarest products are often the most coveted products. This means that if something is like nothing else, it is usually priceless.

The same rarity exists for you and me when it comes to our own value and uniqueness as children of God. Scripture tells us that we are the most unique things that God ever designed. Rare and highly treasured.

The Psalms tell us we are knit together in our mother's womb by God. This means that He takes a very personal approach to shaping our looks, our character, and our soul (Jeremiah 1:4) to craft a person with the utmost uniqueness. I am the most unique being God ever created. So are you.

Being the most unique individual ever to live is tough to wrap my head around. The idea that no other human being past, present, or future will have my same fingerprint is mind-boggling. Think about that for a second. Today, there are about 6.6 billion people on planet Earth.

The website creation.com, a resource that studies the Bible's timeline for how long the world has been around, estimates that Adam and Eve lived around six thousand years ago. You take the 6.6 billion people today and scale that back to the two who lived six thousand years ago, and the resulting number of humans that have lived on this earth over time is in the trillions. Each with a unique fingerprint. Each with a unique design.

This number doesn't even factor those who will come ahead of us in the future. Astonishing! Of all the people that God created past, present, and future, you and I were both created truly unique.

Therefore, uniqueness becomes the core of our creative potential. Recognizing this will allow us to see that being who God made us to be is the first part of stepping into our calling. As we realize our unique value, we will also see that we're called to make, craft, design, and initiate uniqueness as well.

I'm sure you're thinking, *Well that's easy. I know I'm different from everyone else, Luke!* However, it's critical to know this key distinction: being different and being unique aren't the same.

## Coveting Sameness

Identical twins represent this concept so well: looking different isn't the same as being unique. You and I know that they're not the exact same person, but they are often mistaken as the same person if someone wasn't aware they are a twin. But we know twins aren't the same. They carry a unique makeup of DNA. They may not be outwardly different in appearance, but they are truly unique nonetheless.

Being different is a recognition of our outward appearance. Being unique is recognition of our inward design. It's easy to recognize our differences from someone else and never fully harness the uniqueness we were each designed to reflect. Because even though culture at large may celebrate uniqueness through patents and trademarks, we as individuals covet sameness.

Think about the "Joneses." You know, the family that everyone is trying to keep up with? They are that influential family on our neighborhood block. They pull into their driveway with a brand-new car and suddenly our car is out of date. It's no longer reliable. We can't fit the kids in the car we have. We *must* have what they have. Subconsciously we need a new car, because we want what others have.

Maybe the Joneses in your life aren't a literal family next door, but instead they're someone in your friends group or someone you work with. Regardless, everyone in culture has a Jones.

Our covetousness toward sameness drives corporations to pay a pretty penny in celebrity endorsements. Beyoncé appears in Pepsi commercials, and all of a sudden you're thirsty. LeBron James wears a new pair of Nike shoes, and instantly we need new kicks. It's like clockwork because what we want is sameness with those we idolize or respect.

In 2016, *Forbes* magazine posted a list of athletic endorsement deals (sports personalities alone), detailing the amount of money each product or association paid to play into the covetousness of sameness paradox that is so prevalent in our society. The total amount spent in 2016 alone was just under $1 billion.[5]

Our insatiable desire to keep up with the Joneses not only costs these companies a lot of money every year, it costs you and me the ability to see our high-value uniqueness as well. When we only see differences on the outside and celebrate those who have what we want, we give in to a desire for sameness. In doing so, we never see the true uniqueness that is written on each of our souls within.

## Becoming an Image Bearer

In 2012, I spent a considerable amount of time studying scripture as it related to creativity. I wanted to create a biblical foundation for creative process and creative theory. It was a powerful season of my life viewing the Bible through the lens of creativity—seeing all that God has in store for His beloved children who create things on a regular basis.

During that time, I remember studying the first chapter of Colossians, where Paul writes that God made all things for Christ. But not just the things we know of or we see, literally *all* things. He writes:

"[Christ] is the image of the invisible God, the firstborn over all creation. For by him all things were created: things in heaven and on earth, visible and invisible, whether thrones or dominions or rulers or authorities–all things were created through him and for him. And he is before all things, and in him all things hold together."[6]

I don't have enough pages in this book to break down all the theology that lives within those three powerful sentences, but I want you to go back and count the number of times we see the word "all" in there. Five. There's no question that Paul was making a point that all things were for Christ, by Christ, in Christ, and through Christ. And that list of "all things" includes creativity.

Creativity is not for you. It's for Christ. Creativity isn't accomplished by you. It's by Christ. Creativity isn't within you. It's within Christ. And creativity isn't something done through you. It's all accomplished through the being of Christ. But we try to take credit all the time, don't we?

It's important to realize that God designed us in His image so that we would become image bearers of His characteristics. We are not to take credit for the things that were designed for Him but to use those characteristics to create things of infinite beauty to point people back to His story and His glory.

## Prophet or Provider

God's will for our lives is for us to become His image bearers in the world (Genesis 1:27). If creativity is such a large factor of His image, then we must amplify the prophetic side of creativity far more than the service provider side. Let me tell you a story to help illustrate the difference between these two sides to creativity.

When Orange Thread first got started, we produced video content for a variety of clients on a project-by-project basis. I was walking a fine line between company and freelancer back then. The hopeful entrepreneur within me never wanted to be identified as a freelancer, or an individual who comes in for a specific project as contractor but doesn't work full time for the team.

The reason it was a fine line was that Orange Thread was just me when I got started. I provided a quote to a client based on the number of hours I planned to spend on the project, and that number directly correlated to the overall cost to the client. As a freelancer, you're usually paid for your time on a project. And that is why I always seemed to fight the term freelancer when starting out.

I regularly told clients to make sure they paid Orange Thread Media LLC, and I made sure my email address, business cards, quotes, and invoices all had a consistent brand. This was a problem I faced for a year or more. Projects were valued by the time spent.

One day, when talking to a good friend, I had the revelation that the biggest difference between a company and a freelancer was how they budgeted their projects. Since a company will often have numerous people working simultaneously on a project, it's nearly impossible for most of them to charge directly for the time it takes to put a project or product together. Instead businesses charge for the value they provide, rather than the time they expend.

This is why coffee shops are successful. They can pay a barista fifteen dollars an hour to make lattes and charge a customer seven dollars for that cup. It doesn't cost the company half an hour of their employee's time, but it is valued at saving the customer that amount of time (or more). A high-end coffee shop can charge that much because of the value it provides.

That was a pivotal day for me, and it ultimately allowed me to realize what was limiting my growth as a company. From there I started looking at every estimate or quote I wrote based more on the value that it may provide a customer, rather than the time it may take myself or my team. If the value isn't worth the time, we don't quote it out. If the value is worth more than the time, it's a win-win position for both us and our clients.

If I were to apply this to my own creative journey, too often I thought I was merely a service provider with my talent and gifts. I diminished my own creative ability by thinking that I was reduced to the mere amount of time I spent on something, and that the knowledge, skill, insight, and vision I had wasn't worth anything.

However, when I started to see that my creativity was more than just my time, and instead I began pouring my entire creative and technical abilities into a project, I was able add prophetic creativity into the project. By seeing the difference between time and value, I became more like a prophet than a provider and I began to step into my own uniqueness.

My friend Glenn Packiam, lead pastor at NewLife Church Downtown, said this at our 2014 SALT Conference:

> "Our creativity isn't unique because of its form, but because of its prophetic function ... In the Bible, there are two Hebrew words for 'prophet.' The first one means *to see*. And the second one means *to say*. [Therefore,] A prophet is one who sees and says because they see a different world and say a different word. Everyone around them sees one thing, but a prophet sees something totally different."[7]

Being a creative prophet means speaking life into a project that has no vision. It means bringing something into existence that didn't have an existence before. But without knowing your own uniqueness, and creating from the place within you that God designed from nowhere, how can you be the creative prophet that others need?

I must mention that there's nothing wrong with providing a service. Culture needs much more than just a service though. Notice I was limited in investing all of myself when I was only charging for time? Instead, when I charged on value, I could invest every ounce of me in the entire project, and our work became exponentially better. A creative who sees themselves merely as a service provider will merely accomplish the task with the least amount of resistance possible. A creative prophet will accomplish the task by adding the maximum amount of value possible, regardless of the resistance.

No matter the project, the product, or the idea, the *service* of creativity is still a required element in almost every organization.

Ads need to be *designed*.

Videos need to be *created*.

Events need to be *produced*.

Stories need to be *written*.

Moments need to be *made*.

Art is a conduit. It's a pipeline of communication. We need art, creativity, and imagination to carry ideas in a way that cuts through all the cultural noise. But if we resort to being merely a service provider, we rob ourselves of the opportunity to step into our full creative potential. By harnessing the uniqueness written on the soul of each and every one of us, we can walk into creative meetings in a manner that maximizes prophetic creativity.

## Created to Create

It's imperative to know the difference between being a prophet (prioritizing value over time) and a provider (prioritizing time over value) because it helps us see ourselves as who God made us to be. Just as God was creative, we embody the characteristics of creativity as well because we're made in His image. However, I've met countless individuals who don't recognize that term "creative" as part of their own uniqueness, often because we've made creativity and art too synonymous. They are, in fact, very different.

Take my friend Gabby, for example. Just the other day she and I got into the conversation of creativity, and she said to me, "I don't think I'm creative like you guys" (referring to the SALT core team).

Gabby works for an architectural firm. Her team lays out the design of various buildings in our area. They create master development plans to help future architects, builders, or construction crews know where to place future developments. And yet she doesn't think she's creative because of an unrealistic definition that creativity is making something out of nothing.

As an outsider, it's easy to see that Gabby is creative because of the work that she does. But I'm not trying to argue that we are creative because of any outward appearance. That's being different. Instead I'm saying that she's uniquely creative because of who she is on the inside. On the inside, she's a child of God, because her creativity comes from the unique fingerprints that God has designed within her as she expresses God to others in her own voice.

You may not have crafted an award-winning film, penned a chart-topping song, or released a *New York Times* best-selling novel, but none of that is a prerequisite to be an image bearer of Christ. Your being made by God makes you an image bearer of Christ. It's the *being* you are, not the *work* you do, that defines you as uniquely creative.

In this first principle, I want us to recognize that we were made by God, with purpose, and destined to be creative. Our purpose is far greater than just to survive but to instead thrive as we embody the characteristics of God that were designed to touch and transform our communities.

When we ignore the giftedness that defines our uniqueness, we rob God (and ourselves) of our creative potential. We indirectly tell God that we don't want the parts of Him that He gave us, and in turn, fall into the trap of coveting sameness like everyone else in our culture. In doing so, we never step into our

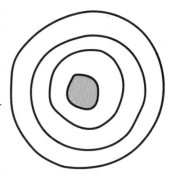

infinite worth, which is summed up by our overwhelming uniqueness.

Recognizing our uniqueness is the first step in establishing our creative Gobstopper. It's the innermost layer because uniqueness represents the core of who we are. Our core is our identity. Our identity is in Christ. Our

Christlike creativity allows us to uniquely operate in a world that covets sameness.

Knowing we are unique is only the beginning. For me, I had to find a series of processes to help break away from the lie that I wasn't creative. I needed a plan to get me out of my covetousness of sameness. Essentially I couldn't just rely on the why of uniqueness; I needed a firm how. So let's get into the process of becoming unique and finish establishing the core of our Gobstopper so we can reach the full potential God has for us.

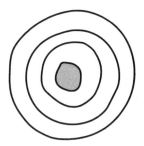

## CHAPTER EIGHT

# Becoming Unique

I'll never forget the most awkward sermon I've ever heard.

One Sunday, I walked into church like I usually did, and everything seemed to go according to plan. Virtually every Sunday of the past two years, the church service followed a template.

The band would begin. The worship leader would give a welcome. The team would sing three or four songs, and the worship leader would pray. During the prayer, the stage manager would bring out the lectern for our pastor. After the prayer, the congregation would sit. The pastor would walk on stage and begin his sermon. He would finish, and we would be dismissed.

However, this one Sunday, things were a bit different. The worship leader prayed, then told us to take our seats. The stage manager brought out the lectern and the lights came up. But the pastor wasn't there.

For a second, I wondered if I was part of some *Left Behind* scene where Kirk Cameron was left behind after the rapture of Christ. How could the pastor not have shown up for his own sermon? Maybe he snuck out to get a coffee and got stuck in traffic trying to get back in time. This was the fourth service after all. Maybe he got stopped in the hallway talking to a member of our church. Whatever it was, it was starting to become awkward as we sat in our chairs, silent.

Thirty seconds turned to a minute. A minute turned to three minutes. The time seemed to slow to a snail's pace, and we waited to see who would come out and apologize for this unsettling delay.

Then all of a sudden we heard something. A whisper through the sound system. The congregation, which had started to talk among themselves, quieted in a moment's notice. We were alert now.

Then it happened again. This time we heard what was being said: "I don't want to speak."

The whisper repeated.

Every whisper caused heads to become periscopes in the quest to locate where the whisper was coming from. Some embraced the mystery; others grew frustrated.

"I don't feel like getting up there," the voice repeated.

At this point in time, I realized, along with many in the room, that our pastor was sitting toward the back of the auditorium in the congregation. He was talking to the person to his right while his microphone amplified what he was saying so everyone could hear.

"I don't want to get up there and speak. I don't feel like it," he said as he stood up, finally relieving the pregnant pause that had developed over the last ten minutes.

As he walked toward the front of the room, my pastor then took the most awkward moment and turned it into one of the most powerful sermons I've ever heard by saying these words:

"When you and I ignore the God-given gifts in our lives, we hinder the spiritual growth of those around us. Because our gifts are not for us but for the benefit of those around us."

As awkward as that moment was on that odd Sunday morning, my pastor showed me firsthand what it meant to be hindered by someone not stepping into the fullness of their own uniqueness. In this chapter I want to break down the process of becoming unique, to help you step into the fullness of your own creative potential and never be placed in the position of hindering the spiritual growth of those in your own community.

## Finding Your Uniqueness

The first step is to identify what it is that makes you unique. In a practical sense, what is the specific gift that God has given you? A few obvious examples include design, story, writing, or technological engineering. But the not-so-obvious examples are strategy, relationships, data analysis, or even administration. All of these require a great deal of creativity and can set you up for a variety of careers.

Some of you know what you're good at. For others, it may take a little bit of time to uncover your specific gift.

But let's look at a few tangible things you can do to hone your unique gift, talent, or ability.

## Pray

The first step is simply asking God to reveal your gifts. As I shared in Act I, I've never prayed and heard an audible voice. But God does answer the prayers of His children.

Remember my trip to Atlanta? I carved out some time to specifically determine if God's plan for my life was to start a youth camp, but He made it very clear with those three questions that my gift in the world was to start a conference instead. Prayer was what gave me this clarity. It's not just a good idea, it's essential. Trying to figure out your gifts without prayer is like trying to become an image bearer of Christ without Christ.

Spend a few minutes each day over the next few weeks specifically praying over your creative calling. Ask God, in bold ways, to make His plans and purpose known to you. As you do, your heart will receive what God is doing in and around your life as it pertains to your uniqueness. This will help you home in on the exact giftedness that God has designed for you to bear as it pertains to His image.

## Ask

Those who know you well will be able to help you identify your true giftedness. So ask someone around you and get insight from those who love you best because they have an outsider's perspective. When you explore what others have to say, specifically ask five groups of people: family, friends, co-workers, your boss, and lastly yourself.

We start with family because they have known you the longest and likely can see the hand of God on your life in order to identify the most growth. For some, your family doesn't see the world through the lens of God, so there may be a temptation to avoid a conversation like this, but I want to encourage you to still ask your family. Regardless, I am almost certain your family loves you. And that's why we start with them because regardless of what you do or who you are, they will give you a safe answer.

Sometimes your friends see you in a different way than family does. And if you're like me and live in an entirely different state than most your family, friends will have a perspective that's entirely different. Like family, they will tell you the truth because they care more about who you are than what you do.

As you move to those you work with, it's good to start with co-workers. They know you in a professional environment and can speak directly to the gifts and abilities they see on a regular basis. Co-workers give more vocational validation because friends and family typically see you in social environments.

I also encourage you to talk to your boss (or a mentor) about your giftedness. They likely decided your salary based on your giftedness and have insights to what you harness that can impact the world. It's also to your boss's advantage for you to find your optimal giftedness.

As weird as it may sound, it's imperative to ask yourself as well. What are you most passionate about or well gifted in? What are the skills that have come naturally to you over the years? What skills were so easy to learn that you forgot how second-nature the training was? What areas do you not have to try so hard to be good at?

Odds are good that several of these groups will overlap somewhere. This overlap in responses will give you a hint at where your giftedness may lie.

## Observe

After we've spent some time praying and asking those five groups, it's time to observe in the waiting. Finding your uniqueness won't come to you overnight. As you may remember in my own story, this took years. I had two stuck starting gates, and it wasn't until those three questions in Atlanta that I could truly observe that my influence was not in the youth ministry world.

I believe there are two key things we must observe in this process: passions and frustrations.

As far as passions go, where do they collide with the world's greatest needs? It may help to do a passion audit during this process. Every time you hear someone in your community say they could use something (anything at all), write it down. It may be that they need new teachers at the local elementary school, or it could be that they need a new park for the community.

On the other page, write down every single time you come up with an "I love doing ... " phrase and put down the specific topic. It can be as simple as "I love helping people" or as complex as "I love engineering the wiring infrastructure for complex technical environments."

As you take a few weeks to observe, find the overlap between areas of needs in the community and passions you have. You'll be amazed at what will come to you over several days. You'll also have a giant list of ways to impact your community and places of your optimal interests.

But after you observe your passions, it's also good to identify those areas that get you most frustrated. Burning frustration propels people to action.

Bill Hybels, lead pastor at Willow Creek Community Church, calls this *holy discontent*. Almost every time I've seen him teach on this principle, he uses the illustration of *Popeye the Sailor Man* as a way of communicating effectively.

If you've ever seen the show, you know the storyline that appears every time. Popeye is a sailor who is traveling the seven seas with his girlfriend, Olive Oyl. She always gets the attention of others, particularly other guys. When these guys in Popeye's camp pick on Olive Oyl, Popeye quickly gets fed up.

This is where Popeye's famous catch phrase came to be: "That's all I can stands, I can't stands no more." Then he opens a can of spinach and downs it on the spot. His biceps immediately bulge from the injection of protein, fiber, and zinc, causing him to beat the living daylights out of those picking on Olive Oyl.

As Hybels has explained, holy discontent is that moment in your life where the situation in which you've found yourself brings such frustration that it leads you to immediate action. A moment that you just can't "stands" anymore! This moment is what Hybels calls the "Popeye moment."

Observe over the next several weeks if you find yourself in Popeye moments of holy discontent—places where you may want to resort to action to solve an injustice or simply fix a problem that is so obvious to you. Within those Popeye moments, you may find clues to where your unique giftedness lies.

As you observe both, let me encourage you with something I found in my own life. Just because you are passionate about something doesn't mean it will always be easy to accomplish. Desire doesn't equate to prosperity.

Persevere. Hang in there when the going gets tough. Every successful person who has uncovered their God-given uniqueness has had to persevere.

## Give

By no means do I want you to think there's a prescription to finding your uniqueness. For me, and from my story, I take these key factors out as building blocks for you to begin to find your own foundation in Christ. And the final element for me to truly know if the conference was what God was inviting me into was to participate in giving.

You know the most famous scripture in the whole Bible, right? John 3:16: "For God so loved the world that he gave his one and only Son, that whoever believes in him shall not perish but have eternal life." Did you catch the key word? It's *gave*.

God gave to us long before He ever asked us to give in return. And just like God did with Abraham and Isaac, sometimes giving is essential to truly know our hearts. I want to encourage you to consider two primary ways you can give as ways to ensure that you're stepping into your true uniqueness. The first is giving of your time.

For me, this was in the form of volunteering. It was one of the first ways I knew that God was asking me to serve in the creative and technical areas of the church. Serving took money off the table as the "incentive," and instead my serving was making me more like Christ.

I don't know why, but money always clouds true success. Since God never says in scripture that your gift will earn you a multitude of worldly wealth, then I think it's important for us to find a way to make sure our giftedness isn't dictated by worldly wealth. If you and I can find our uniqueness without a bank account or profit and loss statement telling us we're successful, then we're on the right track to becoming like Christ with our uniqueness and we avoid any temptation from a performance-based mindset that fuels our perception of success.

Growing up, my dad always taught me to never worry about money because if you do what you love, money will always come. I've come to take this amazing wisdom one step further. If you chase money with your job, you'll rarely see the positive impact your career has made on someone's life. However, if you chase making a positive impact on people's life, you'll rarely have to worry about money.

There's another thing God asked me to give before I was truly able to step into my calling. All throughout my life God has spoken a belief that to grow, we need to let go. And the conference was no different.

Just like Abraham had to be willing to let go of Isaac, you may be called to let go of your own gift or dream to know where your heart lies. I've long wondered if the reason we got another "wall" when we met with my home church about having the conference there was because I wasn't willing to give up this idea before God insisted I give it up.

Maybe it helps to think of this form of giving as a sabbatical from your calling. A time to carve out and re-center on your relationship with God. Because I know firsthand that the passion of a calling can rob you of worship toward God. In the end, I don't believe we're giving up anything when we give up our dreams. We're letting go of the things that will hold us back to gain all that God wants to give in return.

Take some time to pray, ask, observe, and give for a few months as you find your unique giftedness. Pour out whatever you've put in your own cup so that God can begin pouring more of Himself in, and you'll find that eventually His purpose is overflowing over your cup.

## Confidence in Your Calling

Now that you've found your uniqueness, it's time to begin harnessing the power within that uniqueness. With that in mind, my experience has taught me three steps to finding confidence in my calling.

The first is to **stop copying and start creating**. If we can stop seeing the work of others as something we covet for ourselves (remember that "covetousness of sameness" principle), we begin to create truly unique things.

When an artist first starts learning how to draw, they will often use tracing paper to get down the key technique on how to move the pencil or brush. But no great artist has ever changed the world because they knew how to trace another artist's work. To reach our potential, we can't rely on tracing paper in our daily lives.

As we see things that inspire us, we must fight the urge to copy the thing that we were so impressed by in the first place. In doing so, we'll prevent the inevitable library of knockoff ideas and replica creations. Rather than stealing an idea, let it be the grounds for inspiring a new thing within you. In doing so, we see other works of art not as something to steal, covet, or copy but rather as building blocks for future ideas.

Creatives who have found their uniqueness are those who recognize inspiration always breeds inspiration; ideas always lead to new ideas. So don't get caught up in that one idea, but know there are many more as it inspires us to create again.

The second step in this process is to **stop comparing and start creating**. Once we've seen other works as a source of inspiration, our natural tendency is to begin comparing our works to every other creative work. And that's a dangerous place to be. Every time we compare, we allow the voice of the enemy to come in and rob us of our intended potential. The enemy tells us that we're not good enough or smart enough, or on the flip side, he may play into our ego, trying to tell us we're too good to be considered equal to another.

Living with a mindset of continual comparison will turn your community of support into a community of competition. Encouragement turns to opposition. You'll find yourself in fear that someone is becoming better than you, and then stop spending time with them as a personal defense mechanism. This line of thinking will steal your uniqueness and send you down the road toward complete isolation.

Comparison is so deadly to the creative soul and your creative potential that we must setup safeguards in our life to avoid it. A great way to do this is by encouraging more creatives around you.

Go to your Instagram feed and find two people—one you admire and one a bit behind you, creatively speaking. Leave a comment for **both** people encouraging them in their own uniqueness or supporting their creativity.

Encouragement is a vessel of change. You'll not only find that it changes and benefits the people you encourage, but it changes you in the process. It will change you because celebrating the works of others is the antidote of comparison. Encouraging others and the absence of comparison to one another is the foundation of a healthy creative community.

As we'll learn in the unfolding chapters, creativity was never meant to be done in isolation, so fostering this community isn't just a beneficial idea, it's a fundamental idea. As you begin to recognize your uniqueness, do everything you can to avoid the comparison trap, and start being an encourager to those around you.

The third step in the process of becoming unique is to **stop commercializing and start creating**. Once you've overcome the hurdle of copying and fostered an environment of encouragement over comparison, the next part of creativity we must overcome is the desire to package and ship out the same creativity over and over. It happens all the time, often without intention. We use creativity to sell a product or get something to a customer, and to leverage its impact, we package it together and mass produce it.

It's natural to repeat what seems to work. So when you find that a specific style resonates with people, an approach converts well, or a room full of people always respond to a specific creative moment, it's our instinct to employ repeat use.

From graphic design to promo videos, event templates to music, the natural tendency for creativity is to fit a mold that works and franchise it. At its essence, the reason commercializing creativity is so dangerous is that it takes *you and me* out of the creation process and puts a manufactured assembly line into place.

When things become commercialized, there's no room for creativity. Challenging the status quo becomes frowned upon, and the institutional process of getting things out at the lowest cost removes the need for your uniqueness.

Commercialization is dangerous because it removes the need for creativity, and removing the need removes the use. Because creativity is a muscle, its strength diminishes when it's not worked out regularly. Just like you'll never be able to see defined biceps if you don't regularly lift weights, the same is true with creativity. If we stop using it, we lose it. Commercializing creativity may cause you to lose the very uniqueness you're trying to exploit through that assembly line of mass production.

When we franchise creativity, we steal from our future self. We create a dependency on a process rather than the prophetic that we talked about in the earlier chapter. In the end of commercialization, we resort to becoming a service provider with the least possible resistance.

## The Teacher Who Changed My Creativity

Ms. Kylie Dayton was one of my design professors when I was in school. She had years of experience as a designer. Having worked with several creative firms to make collateral pieces (letterhead, business cards, envelopes, etc.) and advertising material (magazine ads, newspapers, billboards, etc.), she carried a lot of weight when it came to a philosophy of design.

One day she said something to our class that has forever changed my outlook on creativity: "Everything has already been designed."

She didn't say it to destroy our hopes of making anything new, but to remind us that creativity is less about innovation and more about iteration.

Innovation is making something out of nothing and creating something that has never been seen. Iteration is taking an idea that already exists to the next level or next dimension as it applies to the context of its environment. Iteration builds on the previous thing; innovation starts from scratch.

When you and I step into our unique creative expression, we should be more concerned with pushing the creative limits, rather than trying to find some never-before-used technique or style.

CREATIVITY IS LESS
INNOVATION AND
MORE ITERATION.

#CREATIVEPOTENTIAL

Remember, we are made in the image of God. An image cannot be 100 percent original and still reflect the thing it is the image of, which means you and I are less innovative unique creations and more iterative unique creations. We resemble the original, which means we're connected in some part to characteristics of something that's already been created. If God, in creating us, leaned more toward the iteration factor than the innovation factor, then we put too much pressure on ourselves to try and always create an innovative solution. Being unique is always in the context of the environment in which you're creating. We don't need to imagine a brand-new thing when everything has already been designed.

Survey the environment God has placed you in. Then create iterations to move people closer to God through your uniqueness. Release yourself from feeling inadequate because your ideas aren't original enough or innovative enough. Innovation is simply an unrealistic goal, when God only ever asks us to create within the context of our surroundings.

What is the uniqueness God is calling you to step into? As I've mentioned before, finding and discovering your uniqueness is the foundation for unlocking your creative potential in the world. If it's not the core of your being, the platform in which the other principles can rest, then you will never fully reach *your* potential. Instead you'll constantly find yourself trying to reach someone else's potential.

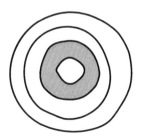

## CHAPTER NINE

# Excellence: Perfect Is a Myth

Now that we have a foundation of uniqueness, it's time to explore the next layer of that Gobstopper: excellence. Our culture wants us to believe the lie that excellence is only achieved when you are the best that exists. This is a lie because this definition of excellence is oxymoronic and not possible.

If to be excellent one must exclusively become the best, then the moment one achieves that status, "best" has a new metric. Can you see that the culture's angle of excellence is a constantly moving target? The result is an evolving definition that anyone intelligent would conclude is not achievable. There can't be a best if there's always a changing best.

In this ever-evolving definition of excellence, creativity becomes a constant process of striving and straining that's not sustainable. It causes us to fight hard for an outward appearance of perfection that dilutes our uniqueness. Which causes excellence to need others acceptance.

Maybe we need to shed the worldly perspective of excellence and begin seeing excellence the way God sees it. In chapter 7, I shared with you the "all things" passage where Christ is the originator of all creative things. In just a few chapters later in the book of Colossians, Paul writes two bold statements:

> "Whatever you do, whether in word or deed, do it all in the name of the Lord Jesus, giving thanks to God the Father through him."[8]
> "Whatever you do, work at it with all your heart, as working for the Lord, not for human masters."[9]

Excellence is not a pursuit of perfect, but instead it's a posture of the heart. God measures our work and the quality of our work by a heart factor, not some concocted perfection factor. You and I must resist measuring our creative excellence with a measuring stick that God doesn't recognize and instead see our creativity and excellence with the same tool He uses: the heart.

## The Excellent Way

Let's look at another book of the Bible that Paul wrote, 1 Corinthians. At the end of chapter 12, we find this amazing statement: "I will show you the most excellent way."[10] It's a setup to the very next paragraph. And those who know 1 Corinthians 13 know what's coming next. It's a giant pre-cursor on how to love people well.

This isn't all that surprising since God measures our creative excellence by the posture of our hearts. And it's fitting that He would also use Paul to say that the most excellent way to live is one with love. These two things go hand in hand. As counterintuitive as it may seem, God's view of excellence is less about doing and more about being. It's how we posture ourselves in light of His goodness.

Therefore I believe excellence is the second layer to that proverbial Gobstopper of creative potential. If the

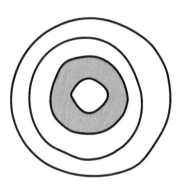

principle of being unique is trying to find yourself, then excellence is being the best you you can be. This means recognizing that to be excellent in God's eyes, it may be choosing to live in a manner that's countercultural. Here are a few examples of what I mean:

Excellence may mean doing less to become more.

Excellence is being real rather than always trying to be right.

Excellence is being vulnerable rather than seeming perfect.

Excellence is having allegiance toward heaven over trying to win the applause of people.

## Satan's Lie

Satan has never created anything.

Look at Genesis. There's no doubt in my mind that God created all things on heaven and earth, which means we can't take our creative insight from someone who has never created a single thing. That would be like trying to learn how to swim from someone who have never been near water. That's insanity. Therefore, we can't model creativity after the lie that Satan is giving us.

Every season of creativity I enter, I find that Satan is trying encourage me to "stop, steal, and borrow" so I will be perceived as perfect in someone else's eyes. He's used every sort of doubt, fear, and insecurity to show me how far from perfect I am. But I can't let him do this, because his only hope is that I stop any attempt from creating. And in stopping my desire to create, the enemy steals my ability to become the image bearer of a creative God.

If Satan wants to stop you from being the best mirror of God's glory, pointing people back to God with your creative potential, then the best way he'll do that is to increase your desire to look like the rest of the world. It's imperative that we understand Satan's lie. God created us in His image, and to be image bearers, we create out of that reflection. Satan will do almost anything to make us believe his lie that we're far from perfect. This will send us down a path of trying to pursue worldly perfection to prove this lie is false. Satan cares about image, the outward difference, but remember God is in love with our true uniqueness.

I like to think of combatting the enemy this way: Every time I create something, I am using my creative abilities to take one small step closer to being like God. Therefore, creativity is a sword in the spiritual warfare going on around us.

I'm certain that the enemy wants you to listen to his lies so he can prevent you from seeing your full potential of using your own abilities to point people back to God. Satan knows that when we create from a place of freedom rather than trying to be like something else, we're channeling a characteristic of God and proclaiming Him as the desire of our heart. This is an act of worship. Creating as a posture of the heart, out of love, is worship that gives God the greatest glory.

No one can buy your love and adoration—that's something freely given from the individual, which is probably a hint as to why God believes excellence is something to do with the heart. Because the purest, most beautiful, and most excellent things we create come from our hearts, as an expression of who God made us to be.

God delights more in the you that you are than the you that you want to be. So our striving, straining, and stressing to be like anything else is out of line with our God-ordained purpose and potential for our lives.

## More through Less

One of the greatest threats to creativity is our perpetual busyness. The constant motion prevents an opportunity to meditate. Think about your typical week. How much time do you have to just let a thought percolate in your mind? Probably not often. And even if you do have time in your schedule where you get to just think, it's likely that this is the most protected and fought for time of your week.

Something amazing happens when we stop for a second and still our minds. When we take a moment, and decide to do less for a moment, we gain the capacity to do more when we return. Rest is a very biblical concept. Jesus spoke about it numerous times, most specifically because the Jewish leaders mistakenly tried to use the Sabbath against Jesus numerous times.

One of my favorite examples is Mark 2:27, when Jesus says to the Pharisees, "The Sabbath was made for man, not man for the Sabbath." The appearance of rest isn't enough for God. It's not some cop-out that we stop for a second and let ourselves take a breath.

I have a love-hate relationship with the word "hustle." The part I love is when it refers to the "make it happen" sort of attitude, where we don't waste time and persevere through tough times. However, I despise how Gary Vaynerchuk and others define hustle as this brute force, hero-like mentality where the regular work week is seventy to eighty hours and sleep is for sissies. This is a striving mentality that I believe isn't what the Bible speaks of. There's nothing wrong with hard work; yes, we all need it. But the hustle of never-ending work is simply not sustainable.

The degree to which we honor rest in our own creative process is the degree to which we honor God. When we place ourselves in a posture of rest, we say with our lives and with our work that we believe God can do more in our less than we can do in our own more. Choosing to do less is an act of worship that shouldn't be overlooked. It's paradoxical because the world doesn't understand the equation that more is less. But God does. He invented that equation.

ONE OF THE
GREATEST THREATS
TO CREATIVITY IS
OUR PERPETUAL
BUSYNESS.

Take Chick-fil-A as an example of the power of this principle. What makes them a token child of this excellence principle is that each of their locations out-perform nearly every other brand in their industry on a per store basis every year. And yet they are closed on Sundays.

A 2015 study by *QSR* magazine (Quick Service Restaurants) found the average Chick-fil-A location earned $500,000 more per year than their closest competitor.[11]

We all know that Chick-fil-A serves great food, but how is it possible that being closed one day of the week allows them to be more successful than everyone in their field? It's because of the biblical principle of less always leads to more. Being closed on Sundays proves that a never-ending, hustle-like striving and straining isn't a requirement to achieve excellence.

When we give into our perpetual busyness and ignore the command of God to rest and give pause to our weekly lives, we basically say to God that we don't need Him in our creative process. Creating this way will always lead to burnout because you'll enter that never-ending spiral of perpetual false improvement toward perfection.

## Our Authentic Posture

Excellence is imperative for our craft to move people. But it must become a personal journey for ourselves, more than an outward quest to impress others. It's a challenge to do less, trusting that God will come through in the more and give us that creative spark. Because everywhere around us, we're encouraged to hustle, try harder, do more, and show a bit more grit.

One of my favorite verses in all of scripture is Psalm 51:16-17, and I love the way Eugene Peterson phrases it in his *The Message* translation:

"Going through the motions doesn't please you, a flawless performance is nothing to you. I learned God-worship when my pride was shattered. Heart-shattered lives ready for love don't for a moment escape God's notice."[12]

God never misses the posture of our hearts ready for love. This means you and I have a choice. We can be fake and go through the motions to create a flawless performance with worldly perfection as our goal, or we can be willing to do less, step into vulnerability, expose our uniqueness, and posture ourselves as the people God created us to be. The path we choose will determine whose praise means more to us: the praise of our Father or the praise of others.

The less we do to make ourselves seem perfect, put together, and flawless, the more we position ourselves in a place of full reliance on who God made us to be. We tap into the sovereignty of God's created purpose and we enter intimacy with Him.

So let's stop pursuing perfection like the world does, and instead rest in the authenticity that God predestined for His people. In that resting, we'll stop allowing ourselves to be filled with the ideologies of the world and let God's truth be the one that fills us up.

We see God's design for our lives is to be in relationship with Him, which means our creativity isn't for us or by us, but rather creativity is a vehicle for God to do something supernaturally through us.

As we give Him our heart, we release the pressure we place on ourselves to be anything but ourselves. If we want to unlock our divine creative potential, we must figure out how to authentically step into the posture of our hearts that showcases the best excellence we can. We don't get caught up in the world's never-ending pursuit of some form of perfection, and we don't give into Satan's lie.

Perfect is a myth because too much of that word has been defined by the world's standards. After all that I have written about that word so far, it may surprise you that Jesus actually says to "be perfect." But we must consider the full context of the verse to recognize why He said it. Look at Matthew 5:43-48:

> You have heard that it was said, 'Love your neighbor and hate your enemy.' But I tell you, love your enemies and pray for those who persecute you, that you may be children of your Father in heaven. He causes his sun to rise on the evil and the good, and sends rain on the righteous and the unrighteous. If you love those who love you, what reward will you get? Are not even the tax collectors doing that? And if you greet only your own people, what are you doing more than others? Do not even pagans do that? *Be perfect, therefore, as your heavenly Father is perfect.*" (*emphasis mine*)

There it is. Jesus telling us to be perfect. But it comes after an entire section of His saying that we aren't to look or act like the world. Instead, we do everything out of *love*—a clue that perfection to God starts with the heart and ends in love. If the heavenly Father is our picture of perfection, then the world's perception of perfect is mythical.

The world's view of perfect is a myth because perfect isn't all that perfect, is it? What I know to be true about these two paths of excellence (posture and pursuit) is that pursuit is exhausting and posture is revitalizing. So why do we continually have to fight the urge to run away from the world's form of perfection? Because it's so different to be truly excellent with an excellence that stems from the heart.

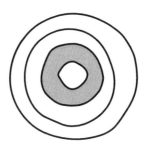

# Becoming Excellent

Now that we have a foundation of excellence, we're ready to look at what it takes to become excellent. This is the next layer of our Gobstopper of potential. However, unlike uniqueness, excellence doesn't have as clear of a process in its becoming. It would be foolish for me to attempt to teach or claim a process that you could *do*, because the Bible has already shown us that excellence is a posture of the heart, rather than the pursuit of a mythical perfection.

There's a natural tension that lies before us as we try to figure out how to be excellent without trying too hard or falling into the previous path of constant effort and striving. So instead I'll spend this chapter laying out a variety of ways that one may become excellent and highlighting for you the characteristics I most often see in excellent people. Before I get into those characteristics, there are two people, both heroes of mine, who will help us establish a few principles of becoming excellent.

## The Peanut Principle

The first man's name is George Washington Carver, and he was born in 1864, right as the Civil War was about to end. Slavery was abolished when G. W. was only a year old, so he was virtually a free man from birth. Being poor and a person of color didn't help G. W. in his quest for the best education he could get regardless of his freedom. But his insatiable curiosity and unending quest for knowledge helped him get into college. Eventually he earned a doctoral degree in agricultural studies to become a certified botanist.

Stories have been written that G. W. went on long walks, where he talked aloud about a multitude of topics. No one ever knew to whom he was talking until his personal journal entries revealed that he was a devout man of God. These were most likely prayer walks to clear his mind and grow him closer to God.

One of my favorite stories about Mr. Carver was one that involved three questions between him and God. The difference between his conversation with God and my conversation was that G. W. was the one who was asking God the questions.

First, he asked God what the purpose of the universe was. Second, he asked God what the purpose of humans were. I've imagined God responded in some fashion of, "Well, those are such big topics, you wouldn't be able to contain all the knowledge of either of those purposes,

George," as if God spoke like a friend walking along the path with G. W.

So the story continues that Mr. Carver asked God one last question. And though it may sound seemingly random, I believe that G. W. knew he had to choose a simple object for God to resolve some of his curiosity. He asked God to show him the purpose of a peanut.

Apparently God granted that request because after his walk, G. W. Carver locked himself in his lab for seventy-two straight hours without letting another soul into the room. When he departed the lab, he departed with him more than three hundred uses for a peanut, most of which he held the patent for years to follow.

Here are just a few of the things he holds the patents for:

**Foods including:**

- Peanut butter
- Pancake mix made from peanut flour
- Coffee
- Chili sauce
- Mayonnaise
- Vinegar
- Butterscotch, and many more

**Everyday household products including:**

- Hand lotion
- Shampoo
- Promade for skin
- Dandruff treatment

- Laundry Soap, and many more

**General inventions including:**

- Paints
- Gasoline
- Writing and printing ink
- Axel grease
- Nitroglycerin
- Shoe polish, and many more[12]

George wanted to know everything there was to know. He had an insatiable desire to learn, followed by a close relationship with the source of all knowledge. So he asked big questions. But God turned him down twice. It was only when he resorted to knowing less that God granted his prayer, filling him with more knowledge than you or I could have ever imagined would come out of a peanut.

What I love about this story is how much it relates to my own experiences. There were three questions and there were two nos before there was a yes. Just because God gives us a no when we want to step into our calling doesn't mean that it is His way of saying never. Don't confuse those two things. Keep investing in the relationship, putting your heart into your work as an overflow of love toward the Creator, and excellence will be the result.

G. W. wanted to make an impact, and I think somewhere along the line God knew that this story would be told, and God would get all the glory. When we put our all into something, and our all is rooted in the being of Christ, it's Christ that shines in all that we do.

The principle we gain from George Washington Carver's story is that God's no does not necessarily mean never, but instead it may mean *not yet*. Keep pursuing God before pursuing the action of the calling. He is the source of all knowledge, insight, and expertise. The key to becoming the best we were made to be is in the being of Christ, not the pursuit of perfection to the world.

## The Spielberg Principle

I believe that Steven Spielberg is one of the greatest directors ever to work in the film industry. He's the Oscar-winning director of *Saving Private Ryan* and *Schindler's List*. He's the mastermind behind nominated films like *Jaws*, *E.T.*, and the *Jurassic Park* trilogy. Anyone who appreciates good film will admit that Spielberg is excellent at what he does.

Spielberg is where our second principle of excellence comes from, and I call it the Spielberg Principle. Simply put: the Spielberg Principle is believing that we can become the best us when we're fully focused on our true gifts. He is a phenomenal film director because he doesn't try to be all things; he does what he's gifted at, and he sticks to a specific genre of movies as well. Nowhere on the IMDB (International Movie Database) is there a single credit for visual effects, acting skills, or composing a film score. There are a few uncredited notes as the "visionary" or the "concept," but at the end of his day, he didn't try to know everything.

Whitney George, pastor at Church on the Move, shared with me on the phone that he believes there's an unhealthy comparison to Spielberg by those who want to be filmmakers in the church. He said that our desire to be like Steven Spielberg is unhealthy because rarely do we put in the time needed to focus our giftedness like Steven has. And Whitney is right!

Steven Spielberg has spent countless hours refining his craft. He's the best because he focused all of his energy, over time, to one specific skillset. I'm not an Oscar-nominated filmmaker because I haven't put in the hours to refine my filmmaking skills. And that's where the principle comes into play. If we want to become excellent, we must stop trying to be all things. Doing less in all areas will allow us to become more in that one area.

There are a few of you who may have become frustrated reading the last few paragraphs because for some reason or another you have a job or a career that doesn't allow that sort of focus. I get it. In our company, and often in the church, team members wear three, four, even five or more hats. It's the paradox of the startup company or any budget-conscious organization.

Here's the best advice I can give to those who wear multiple hats: Own the hat you're wearing in the moment you wear that hat. Don't try and wear all the hats at the same time. Instead, those who take ownership of the situation around them don't wait for others to tell them what to do. They trust that God has gifted them for the hat they are wearing, and they step into excellence from a place of confidence rather than concern of doing too much.

No matter how many hats you are wearing, the Spielberg Principle applies. Focus when you're given the opportunity to focus. If we don't, we'll never wear a single hat, and we'll wonder why we still have to juggle all these different roles sever al years down the road. We will never have found ourselves in a place wearing the hat that we were most designed to wear.

So the second principle of becoming excellent is to put blinders on all the other options out there and find an undying focus for the task at hand. This will allow you to step into more of who you were meant to be.

## Characteristics of Excellent People

Ever since the day I feel like God gave me the word *excellence* as the second layer of the creative Gobstopper, I began a very informal study on what makes someone excellent at what they do. Throughout the course of this ongoing observation on my part, I've seen some trends repeat themselves.

I've found that excellent people must first have **an insatiable desire for personal growth**. Remember we don't learn to become perfect, we learn to be more of who we are in light of God's gift on our lives. Learning doesn't derive from trying to compare or compete. It is healthiest when you have a dissatisfaction of what currently is, or the status quo. This is where the desire for being better stems from.

A great example of this is Tiger Woods. You may think he's the most talented golfer to ever play the game, but I can assure you that this guy has an insatiable desire to get better. In 2006, after he had won two masters and the US Open (two of the largest and most competitive competitions in golf), his team posted his workout routine on TigerWoods.com:[13]

| | |
|---|---|
| **6:30 a.m.** | One hour of cardio. Choice between endurance runs, sprints or biking. |
| **7:30 a.m.** | One hour of lower weight training. 60-70 percent of normal lifting weight, high reps and multiple sets. |
| **8:30 a.m.** | High protein/low-fat breakfast. Typically includes egg-white omelet with vegetables. |
| **9:00 a.m.** | Two hours on the golf course. Hit on the range and work on swing. |
| **11:00 a.m.** | Practice putting for 30 minutes to an hour. |
| **Noon** | Play nine holes. |
| **1:30 p.m.** | High protein/low-fat lunch. Typically includes grilled chicken or fish, salad and vegetables. |
| **2:00 p.m.** | Three to four hours on the golf course. Work on swing, short game and occasionally play another nine holes. |
| **6:30 p.m.** | 30 minutes of upper weight training. High reps. |
| **7:00 p.m.** | Dinner and rest. |

Tiger Woods had a never-ending desire to better himself. Not to win more, he was already winning. I believe it was because of an internal drive to be the best athlete he was designed to be. He was never satisfied with the status quo. He wanted to know what he didn't know. And every time he practiced or stepped onto the driving range, he was saying to himself, "Tiger, there's more to know."

Look at his schedule! He was spending twelve hours straight working on technique and routine practice to become the best golfer he could become. I'll admit that this sort of workout routine leaves very little margin. There's no question that Tiger had an insatiable desire to improve his performance. I believe this is a key characteristic to anyone who is excellent at what they do.

Excellent people also have an **uncanny openness to failure**. They don't fear failure, rather they see it as a catalyst for further development and future opportunity. They see their mistakes as windows rather than walls to their next thing.

Take Steve Jobs and Warren Buffet as prime examples of this characteristic. When Steve Jobs was kicked out of Apple in 1985, he didn't see this as a failure but as an opportunity. So he started a company called NeXT Computers. The name itself signifies the opportunity he saw before him.

During his short tenure at NeXT, they developed innovative ways to lay out the user interface for a computer and revolutionized the physical design. However, NeXT itself was another major failure for Steve Jobs. Reports show it had over $50 million in debt at their peak. It's as if this didn't faze Jobs. He seemed to know failure would lead to success if they kept seeing failure as another way of learning.

Eventually Apple reached back out to Steve Jobs, asking him to return to Apple. With his return, he brought the technology of NeXT. Today, the basis of the Macintosh Operating System, named "X," still resembles much of the innovation that was uncovered during the season of NeXT.

Then there is Warren Buffett. As an investing tycoon and one of the world's wealthiest individuals, he didn't get there by avoiding risk. A great example of this is the shoe company called Dexter Shoe that he bought in 1993. He paid $433 million for the company, and after eight years it was worth virtually nothing.

Here's what Warren Buffet said about that decision:

> "I bought a company in the mid-'90s called Dexter Shoe and paid $400 million for it. And it went to zero. And I gave about $400 million worth of Berkshire stock, which is probably now worth $400 billion. But I've made lots of dumb decisions. That's part of the game."[14]

Failure is part of growth. And those who become some of the best of the best know that to be a key principle to live by. Neither Steve Job's $50 million debt or Warren Buffet's loss of $400 million shut them down. They both were empowered by those bad decisions to make better decisions in the future. A character of excellence that will help you reach your full potential is seeing failure as a learning opportunity rather than a closed door to future opportunity.

Third, those who repeatedly achieve excellence **don't let others define their metric of success**. There is a difference between ambition and competition. If excellent people are seeing improvement, they don't need others to lose in order to be (or feel) successful. Someone doesn't have to loose in order to excel, because their form of excellence doesn't need other people to define their metric of success.

When I was growing up, I was in competitive swimming. Of all the other sports I played, including baseball, soccer, and tennis, this sport was by far my favorite. I think it has something to do with how winning is defined. Unlike other sports, success in swimming doesn't always mean you get first place. In football, baseball, tennis, soccer, and countless other sports, to win, someone else must lose. But those who have been swimmers on a professional level know this isn't necessarily true because they don't let others define success as much as they allow themselves to define their own success.

Sure, there's a gold medal given to the fastest person at the Olympics in a specific race of swimming, but I believe that's the exception to this rule. For most of swimming, improving your own time is the goal. Instead of racing against others to become the best, you're always trying to race against yourself. The difference may be subtle, but it's powerful when you apply it to your own calling or life.

To be excellent, we must not let others define our metric of success. It's an intrinsic measurement to be one's own best. Instead of a sport where a win also requires a loss, truly excellent people want to pull the best out of everyone around them, and they see a win when everyone wins. Being excellent isn't about competition to them. It's personal ambition that drives them to win. And they're usually for the entire community to be their best as well.

Finally, the most excellent people in the world have unlocked the secret of **hyper-focus and perseverance**. I started the chapter with two men who embody this characteristic beautifully, George Washington Carver and Steven Spielberg. Let me take this one step further though.

We live in a world of constant interruption and distraction. It's tough to stay focused when we constantly have social media accounts to update, messages to respond to, an inbox to attend, and countless alerts and notifications that pop up on nearly every device we own. This doesn't even factor in the common "gotta minute" meetings that seem to pop up throughout any given workday. Think about it: how many times are you with a friend and their watch, phone, or tablet seems to ding, vibrate, or alert them of something "they must attend to right now"?

We live in a world of never-ending access to content. And those I find to be excellent in the world find a way to lessen the amount of content they consume in order to give room to creating their own content.

Studies have shown that it takes the average person twenty-three minutes and fifteen seconds to get back to an unhindered rhythm of productivity once they have become distracted.[15] As one of my pastors says, "Sometimes you need to turn off someone else's reality so you can see the reality God has for you."

That will preach right there! And it's why being so hyper-focused on the person God made you to be is the best way you can embody excellence and increase your creative potential.

There's one more reason you need to learn how to persevere through this process. When you have identified your God-given uniqueness and begin to step into the excellence God indented for you by creating and living out of a posture of the heart, you will gain the attention (if you didn't already have it) of Satan. This newly acquired attention is now a threat from the enemy, who is trying to prevent you from stepping into your creative potential.

You know what this means?

It means war!

But don't let the spiritual battle around your creative calling usher in fear—we know that the war has already been won. We just need to persevere long enough to show the enemy we're not worth his time.

None of this can take place without being intentional with our actions. Turn off your notifications, focus on the hat you're wearing right now, and persevere when it seems that everyone around you needs something from you. When you do this, you'll prevent someone else's priorities from getting in the way of your opportunities by reclaiming your own schedule and increasing your focus. Furthermore, stepping into your calling will show the enemy (and the whole world) that you're made in the image of an infinitely creative God who has purposed you for such a time as this.

## Good + God

As I finish discussing the practical portion of becoming excellent, I hope you've seen some simple yet powerful ways to increase your creative potential by quitting the chase for worldly perfection. But I want you to recognize what will happen when excellence becomes standard in your creativity and how it specifically increases your potential to change the world. It's what I call "Good + God".

Our world champions great art and creativity. Look at Instagram. The posts with the most likes usually include a subject of incredible beauty or a concept that's hysterically clever. We like things that are good! And with so much noise coming from social media, we've become accustomed to tuning out mediocre posts.

I've caught myself from time to time scrolling down my feed quite rapidly because nothing stands out. Good creativity always beckons attention.

Now apply this to reaching the world with our art. If good creativity always beckons attention, then we must ensure the creativity we use for the message of Jesus Christ is also good. We want people to see the God-story in the things we create. But if the things we create aren't good enough, no one will ever see the God in it.

Our mission is to tell a timeless story in a timely manner, and the gospel doesn't need anything added to be effective. However, when we use creativity as a vehicle for this message to be delivered to the world, we must ensure that it's a great medium to carry the greatest message.

In Ephesians 2:10, Paul writes, "For we are God's handiwork, created in Christ Jesus to do good works, which God prepared in advance for us to do." For a while now, the word "good" in that scripture has stood out to me. Why use such a bland word? Why not "excellent works" or "best works"? This would have been a great opportunity to connect back to what Jesus said in the fifth chapter of Matthew when He said "perfect works." But in some peculiar way, Paul uses a word that when translated to English means "good."

If you have a second, go grab your Bible. It will be worth it.

You probably haven't even considered getting up. So I'll precede.

Flip to the very first page of scripture. In Genesis 1, there's a phrase repeated over and over: "And God saw that it was good."

OUR MISSION IS
TO TELL A
TIMELESS STORY IN
A TIMELY MANNER.

#CREATIVEPOTENTIAL

CREATIVE POTENTIAL

Wait, there's that word again: "good." Why would God (who was creating these unbelievable things) call them "good"? Why not say "excellent" or "amazing"?

And that's where it hit me in my own creative journey. Maybe Paul is trying to help us see that God's measure of the things He created is the same good He asks of our own works. It's impossible to think that God's creation is anywhere near mediocre. And this leaves us with a pretty powerful command. We must use good to show people God.

If we reclaim our identity as Christians who live with excellence, then we will likely increase the number of people exposed to the gospel through our creative works. Excellence isn't designed by God to be a never-ending pursuit of worldly perfection, where we stress over unsustainable striving and straining. He's asking us to posture ourselves with a heart that yearns to create good things in response to the good that God has already created. When we do this, we take one more step toward reaching the fullness of our creative potential and see that once again God is pouring into us so that we can have confidence in our calling and maximize our impact.

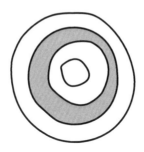

## CHAPTER ELEVEN

# Collaboration:
# We > Me

I've briefly mentioned in previous chapters that creativity can't reach maximum potential in isolation. It's time to focus on that concept even further and begin looking at the process of building a collaborative environment. Collaboration is the third layer of the growing creative Gobstopper to harnessing the fullness of your creative potential.

To fully recognize the power of creative collaboration, we must understand that there are two primary benefits.

First, *we* benefit from collaboration. We benefit from others using their creative abilities and aligning them with our creativity. When we let others into our creative process, they refine and push us to new versions of ourselves. Thus they help us posture our uniqueness to a whole new level.

This benefit is easy to wrap our head around because it's our self that sees growth. We become better people, and our potential is one step closer to its maximum point of impact. Second, *others* benefit from collaboration. We aren't the only ones who can benefit from a truly collaborative environment. Just as others are going to help us, we must also be willing to help others. It's not always going to be what you want to spend your time doing, but look at it as an indirect investment into your own creativity.

Leadership coach Tim Elmore uses a metaphor in teaching this theory of indirect investment. Every time you make an investment in someone else's life, he says to imagine yourself giving the other person a few coins to put in their pocket. Over time, that collection of pocket change becomes valuable. And when you need something in return, you can afford to make a withdrawal.

Creative collaboration is like pocket change, and when you try to benefit yourself without pockets full of valuable coins, then you're up a creek. But when you invest well into other people and help them reach their maximum potential, then you'll have plenty of money to withdraw from when the time comes.

In Exodus, God asks Moses to leave his hometown, travel to Egypt, and tell Pharaoh to let God's chosen people free from slavery. And I forgot, until recently restudying the life of Moses, that he says no to God at first. He wasn't willing to do the work.

In Exodus 4:14, Moses says, "O Lord, please send someone else to do it," after a series of ongoing excuses. Obviously, Moses ends up going, and we know that he effectively convinces Pharaoh to let God's people go, but there was hesitancy to use his gifts for the benefit of other people.

You and I have said this same thing to God over and over: "Please send someone else." And it's important to recognize that this creative collaboration process isn't going to be easy. We're going to want others to do the hard work instead of us. Whenever you're willing to lay down your life, skills, and abilities in the service of others, the kingdom of heaven grows a little bit more. Which means the payoff for creative collaboration is eternal!

Let's not just hope God's kingdom is expanded on this earth, let's do something to help its expansion. Our uniqueness multiplied helps others become the best in their own uniqueness too.

## Trinitarian Creativity

I could spend pages upon pages of this book laying out all the times in scripture that encourage you to work out your calling in the company of others. There are countless moments throughout the Bible where it shows ministry wasn't meant to be attempted alone. But I find in my own story and in the stories of so many others that it's our instinct to be a lone ranger. We perceive that we will gain control and increase our effectiveness if we operate on our own, but that's not the case most of the time. To the detriment of our well-being, operating without a community leads to a quicker burnout and requires more rest after the inevitable fall.

Instead of going through every example in scripture, I want to go to the single most important biblical principle of collaborative creativity, which is the Trinity itself.

If the very essence of God couldn't be contained in one single presence, and instead He felt He would be far more effective with a team of presences, then why in the world do we think we can operate outside of a team?

Matthew 28:19 shows that the Father, the Son, and the Holy Spirit are in fact representing God collectively. It's the bedrock of our Christian theology, the Godhead three-in-one.

When God designed you, He did so with the concept of collaboration in mind. He knitted you together in your mother's womb, He sent His Son to provide a way for you that you couldn't provide on your own, and He has the Holy Spirit as your Helper along the way. It's astonishing that God Himself didn't try to do all of this on His own. God collaborated with Himself to show us our need for collaboration with others.

The entire story of the Bible is the story of God trying to regain the intimacy and relationship that we originally had with Him in the garden, which means his number one priority is being in relationship with you. That in and of itself is a collaborative spirit. And I can't help but think what God imagines when we try to do this thing called creativity, making in the image of our Maker, alone.

Collaboration is a picture of the kingdom of God. It was never God's plan for humanity (or even divinity) to be in isolation from one another.

## A Piece of the Puzzle

An amazing thing happens when you operate as a team or in a collaborative environment: it's near impossible for one person to take credit for the success.

GOD COLLABORATED
WITH HIMSELF TO
SHOW US OUR NEED
FOR COLLABORATION
WITH OTHERS.

Maybe part of the reason God designed us to operate in creative collaboration is to prevent the pride that would arise from isolated success. In the end, God gets all the glory for a collaborative creative project. Remember, all things were created for God.

Of all the scripture that deals with this collaborative principle, my favorite is in 1 Corinthians chapter 12:

> Now there are varieties of gifts, but the same Spirit; and there are varieties of service, but the same Lord; and there are varieties of activities, but it is the same God who empowers them all in everyone. To each is given the manifestation of the Spirit for the common good. For to one is given through the Spirit the utterance of wisdom, and to another the utterance of knowledge according to the same Spirit, to another faith by the same Spirit, to another gifts of healing by the one Spirit, to another the working of miracles, to another prophecy, to another the ability to distinguish between spirits, to another various kinds of tongues, to another the interpretation of tongues. All these are empowered by one and the same Spirit, who apportions to each one individually as he wills.[16]

Notice how Paul starts that whole section: "there are a variety of gifts, but the same Spirit." When it comes to our creativity, collaboration is so vital because when more than one of us get in the room we harness more of the gifts God gives each of us. Therefore, our creativity (through unity) becomes more like the Spirit of God that is within each of us.

I imagine God likes puzzles. I don't have any biblical reference to back up this claim; it's purely my opinion. But I mention that because this scripture causes me to see myself as a piece of a bigger puzzle. Whenever you pick up a single puzzle piece and look at it, you can never see the whole picture. You see a fragment, a glimpse of a specific area, but never the full image.

Maybe you and I are like puzzle pieces in God's grand story. We represent a small piece of His larger narrative, and only when we work with one another in creative collaboration does our puzzle piece lock together with another puzzle piece and we become a beautiful picture. It always takes a bit longer to complete a puzzle, but I've found that it's worth it in the end.

When any of us choose to ignore the principle of collaboration in creativity, it's like taking a single puzzle piece out of the box and throwing it away. The puzzle will never be complete. We need one another. We need each other's gifts and abilities. We may be of the same spirit, but without recognizing each other's collaborative uniqueness at work, our excellence will never be fully revealed, and our creative potential will be crippled.

## Lost in Isolation

Have you ever noticed that ideas seem to come at the most random times? In my experience, there are three common places ideas come to me. I call them the lonely three since you're most likely by yourself without the distraction of other people or devices to interrupt your wandering mind.

The lonely three are: in the shower, on the toilet, and in the car.

You're probably laughing right now because it's so true! Often our most creative moments come to us when we're by ourselves and our mind is given a break. As I mentioned before that creativity is a muscle, these "lonely three" moments are opportunities for your mind to go to the gym. It's impossible to consume content effectively in these three, so it's easier for us to create within our own minds as a result.

But the lonely three aren't just the places ideas are born, sometimes they're the last places that an idea will surface. In the book *Making Ideas Happen*, author Scott Belsky makes this powerful point: "Most ideas are born and lost in isolation."[17] Ideas may come to you in isolation, but he argues an even bigger point. Because you are isolated from others to refine, define, or confine your creative idea, it gets lost like a vapor in outer space.

We need a community around us to make sure that we don't operate in too much isolation, or else our ideas might be lost forever. Just like your muscles grow in between visits to the gym, collaboration is like the rest given to torn muscles that need repair.

Proverbs 27 offers a profound wisdom connected to the spirit of collaboration: "As iron sharpens iron, so one man sharpens another."[18] Typically, when you try to sharpen an object, it takes one hard object and one softer object. Using the harder material, you rub it at a fast but controlled pace, and your softer material loses some of its outer coating, forging a sharper object. When sharpening metal, usually the goal is to have a fine point or edge. Think about it: we don't sharpen things that don't need a point. We sharpen knives and pencils. We sharpen them so they become more effective in their intended use. However, something happens when you choose two hard metals to sharpen together. They can sharpen each other while friction is applied.

Therefore, iron is significant due to its extremely hard chemical makeup. When two people of similar skill and giftedness push toward a common goal to make the other more effective, they become more effective themselves. It is why collaboration is so imperative. In helping others, we ourselves benefit because we learn how to teach. Those who can teach effectively know what it takes to improve their own selves too.

## The Glory of the Wall

Nehemiah has always been one of my favorite characters in scripture. Maybe it's because God used his dreams to change nations, or maybe it's because he's not a prophet or a king but an ordinary guy after God's own heart to do something with his gifts. Regardless, I had an experience a few years ago that deeply impacted my life related to Nehemiah and collaboration.

In the third chapter of Nehemiah, something amazing happens. The writer lists all the families and tribes that helped rebuild the wall of Jerusalem. Reading through this list of people, you realize all the uniqueness that was embraced during that day. A community came together to help fulfill Nehemiah's dream of rebuilding the walls of Israel.

A few years ago, I visited Jerusalem and had a chance to see the walls that surround the city. Throughout the last eighteen hundred years, several areas of the wall have been torn down by various kingdoms and rulers, but a few sections of the wall remain. When I finally found one area of the wall that was built during Nehemiah's time period, what lay before me was remarkable.

The bricks were all the same color as one another. The mortar, seemingly uniform. There was no break where you would have thought numerous people had worked together. It seemed to be one cohesive wall, *not lacking anything.*

And as you read Nehemiah chapter 3, you can't help but see the thousands of people that all worked together to rebuild the wall and imagine that it wouldn't have had one cohesive style. There wasn't one company of brick-layers that built the wall, right? But instead it showed me firsthand that *there is* one company of people laying bricks together—the people of God.

Collaboration is such a beautiful picture of the body of Christ coming together, giving glory to the Creator. Standing there in Jerusalem, looking at the wall Nehemiah built, I couldn't help but think about the countless times I chose isolation over collaboration and robbed God of the glory He deserved.

I'm not advocating that every single time you create there needs to be ten people around you. And I'm not saying that creativity can't happen outside the context of a team. I'm simply saying if you want to reach your maximum potential with your creative abilities, the only way to sustain long-term growth is to find a community of people to be creative with. This community will push you when you need it and remind you that creativity isn't just for your benefit but for the benefit of those around you too.

## Pixar Prosperity

As I close this chapter out, I want to leave you with one final story to show the power of collaboration. I love Pixar. I've seen every single one of their movies. But what's astonishing aren't just the movies themselves but the collective success they've had over the years.

Prior to being purchased by Disney in 2006, Pixar released six feature-length films in theaters. It's important to remember that these six films were the first and only films they had made. Those first six movies were *Toy Story* (1995), *A Bug's Life* (1998), *Toy Story 2* (1999), *Monsters Inc.* (2001), *Finding Nemo* (2003), and *The Incredibles* (2004).

Every single one of those films became the number one film the weekend they were released. Not only that, they all became box-office hits, setting new records for a film studio that didn't have a long history of making films.

This is astonishing—no studio had ever achieved this level of sustained success over such a long period. Even more astonishing is what Ed Catmull, co-founder and president of Pixar, said in 2008 about their culture of creativity: "We have never bought a script or movie idea from the outside. All of our stories, worlds, and characters were created internally by our community of full-time artists."[19]

In a day when most studios were struggling to find the right "idea," Pixar showed that when you work as a team and collectively rely on the collaborative spirit of a unique group of people, success isn't just likely, it is almost predictable.

Catmull doesn't believe their success is luck. And I don't believe they're successful because of only one or two key people. They have more than twelve hundred employees. They have found power in collaboration.

As you begin to step into your own uniqueness, creating out of the heart, the next step is to surround yourself with people who will be like iron in sharpening one another. We is greater than me.

As you find this community, don't be afraid to pour all your own uniqueness into them as you identify ways to help spur them on to even greater things. What I think you'll find in the process is that it's not them who have changed, as much as you'll notice the change in yourself and your own abilities.

Begin by being iron to someone around you. Run from isolation and, in love, help others be more of themselves. It's in this community that you'll find the exponential power of collaboration, and you'll have placed one more layer on your Gobstopper of God-given potential.

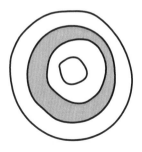

## CHAPTER TWELVE

# Becoming Collaborative

We now have a great foundation for the why behind collaboration and fostering a community of support around us. In this chapter, I'm going to unveil some principles of collaboration that will help us as we explore the rest of that third layer of the creative Gobstopper. If at the core of our creativity is our uniqueness, and becoming excellent is posturing yourself to be the best version of yourself, then collaboration is the multiplication of your potential in the context of community.

We all know the name Lance Armstrong, either for the antidoping charges in 2012 that stripped him of his athletic titles or for his long-standing career in the world of cycling. The man who created those yellow "Livestrong" bracelets is both famous and infamous in modern culture, and regardless of your stance, he is a household name because he will forever be one of the greatest cyclist ever.

You may not be aware, but cycling is not an individual sport. Though our celebrity culture couldn't begin to tell you any of the other names from the United States Postal Service team, there is no question cycling is a team sport.

In cycling, teams deploy two highly collaborative strategies to win. These two strategies are "drafting" and "the slingshot." Through these two strategies, we can gain key insights on how to become collaborative within the community that surrounds ourselves.

**First let's look at drafting**. I found it odd that, in cycling, all the athletes pedal in a straight line. I always thought this was a bad idea because they travel so close to one another they'd likely hit the cyclist in front of them, causing an ill-fated crash. However, this is part of their strategy.

This strategic technique is called drafting. Riders travel nearly on top of one another to benefit from the wind tunnel created by the rider in front of them, thus lessening air resistance. Statistics show drafting can save up to 27 percent of the wind resistance, allowing those athletes not in the front position to get an opportunity to rest.[20]

They call this line formed by cyclists a "paceline." The front man is considered the leader, or "the puller." The leader takes on the wind resistance on behalf of the entire team. And those behind the leader get to tuck their heads down, benefiting from the aerodynamic hole created by the cyclist in front of them. In doing this, all the cyclists beyond the puller gain a substantial amount of reserve energy.

MENTORING IS
NOT *REPLICATING*
YOURSELF,
MENTORING IS
*MULTIPLYING*
YOURSELF.

#CREATIVEPOTENTIAL

When it comes to your own creative journey, I'm not proposing that we model drafting by setting up our desks in a single file line to mimic a cyclist paceline. But that would be funny to see! Instead, the sort of wind resistance we're looking to lessen is the learning curve of our creative abilities by entering collaboration through the models of mentorship and apprenticeship.

Two ways we can strengthen the collaborative environment around us is to be mentored and find someone to mentor. Let's talk about *being* mentored first. When someone else is pouring into you, teaching you from their experience and helping you find your maximum potential, it mimics the model of being one of the second, third, or fourth riders in a cyclist's paceline. In doing so, you learn from the challenges they've faced on their own journey, and you'll be more prepared to face those challenges in your own future.

On the flip side of being mentored is an opportunity to pour out of the glass you have filled over time through the mentoring of someone else. I mentioned at the start of the chapter that collaboration is multiplied potential, and mentoring someone else gives you a practical opportunity to do just that. By pouring yourself into someone else, you find an opportunity to see your own uniqueness carried on as you invest in the next generation or another human soul. Your creative potential becomes a legacy that's passed on to others.

Often, I've resisted considering myself a mentor because I don't believe I have enough to offer. That's because I'm seeing mentoring the wrong way. Mentoring is not replicating yourself; mentoring is multiplying yourself.

My goal in mentoring should never be to create another me, and neither should you. In doing so, we limit the one we mentor. Instead, our desire in mentoring should be to multiply what God and others have taught us, so that we in turn help them start with a foundation of insight much greater than we had when we began. Give the one you invest in an opportunity to start with a better launching pad than you had. Replicating yourself will cause you to think the most they can ever learn is what you have to teach, and nothing else.

There's something powerful in the picture of caring more about the growth of those around us. When we do that, we open our eyes to the reality that life isn't about us. If you've had a successful career or built for yourself a well-established platform, mentoring someone else is essential in keeping you levelheaded.

But most of all, I can speak from personal experience that mentoring someone else will make you better at what you do. Whenever I have had to teach someone a process that I have or equip someone else on the way I go about accomplishing a task, I make way for extraordinary self-evaluation.

Think about it. When you are compelled to teach someone how to do something, you must figure out the most streamlined, effective way to communicate what it is that is required for that task, that topic, etc. Therefore, in teaching someone else to become better, you discover that you also become better at whatever it is you're teaching.

Want to become a better designer? Find someone to teach design to. Want to know the Bible better? Start a

Bible study for young adults. Want to lead better? Pour your insights into a first-time leader.

In cycling, there's another strategy called **the slingshot**. Once a team has been in the same paceline for a while, it's time for the leader to get some much-deserved rest. The way this happens is the first person becomes the second, the second becomes the third, and so forth. To place a new person in the lead, the team must "slingshot" the last player into first place. It's likely that the last person has had the least wind resistance and has more potential energy.

The name is derived from what it looks like when executed correctly. Moving the last player into the first-place position, they must mimic a bungee-like effect. The last rider falls back a few feet, allowing some space between them and the person in front of them. And in a slingshot manner, the trailing rider uses a boost of energy, flying past the team, and landing in the first-place position.

Without the slingshot, the lead cyclist would have to work twice as hard as the rest of the team for the duration of the race. They wouldn't be acting like a team at all. Instead, they take turns being the lead cyclist by slingshotting each rider over the course of the race depending on each cyclist's strengths and the course itself.

You may be able to imagine how slingshots can be employed to maximize the overall speed of the group during a race. This concept proves that a team can travel faster for a longer duration of time—much faster and longer than an individual could because they're able to benefit from each other's abilities and strengths.

When you and I use the slingshot method in our own collaborative environments, it's as if we see every person in our community exactly as they are: unique. And we use that uniqueness to benefit from one another's collective strengths, making the whole better than the individual. I would argue that, even with the allegations of doping that stripped Lance Armstrong of his Tour de France wins, he still would have won numerous times. Lance Armstrong doesn't win merely on his own strength; Armstrong wins because he is part of an incredible team. This is what is so devastating about his story, he didn't even see that principle at work in his career.

It's one thing to be the best you that you were designed to be. But if you want continued success over a long trajectory, you need to find others willing to go through the creative journey with you. When you have a team alongside you, creativity will be amplified because there's a community of people drawing ideas out of each other, slingshotting each other's unique gifts.

## Where Collaborative Exists

Since collaboration has a multiplying effect, there are three practical places in which collaboration is something we must work on.

**First, we must see one-to-one collaboration.** Think of this as a partnership, but it's often with the co-workers who serve on the same team as you. These are the people who have similar skill sets and who work with you from day to day. Earlier I wrote about the indirect investment in the context of pocket change, where one-to-one collaboration is a direct investment in others.

For some of you it's a fellow designer. For others, it's one who complements your creativity. For those who volunteer with your gifts, it may be another person on your volunteer team. When we collaborate with someone on a one-on-one basis within our own team, we increase our chances of learning another area organically and making the team a better, more well-rounded group of individuals.

You've probably heard the phrase "you're only as good as your weakest link." Collaborating on a one-to-one basis within your own team helps make sure that everyone is operating at their best, which means your collaborative efforts have a direct link to the overall strength of the team.

When we work with others, we don't limit the understanding of our role to the tasks we're responsible for, but instead see the fuller picture of what our team needs to accomplish. Perspective is key in any organization that wants to find its rhythm. If you can't collaborate within your own team, it will be strenuous to collaborate effectively elsewhere.

**Next, we must find organizational collaboration.** Some teams don't have departments, but almost all teams have a few areas of focus. Let's take my team as an example.

We currently have three primary divisions at Orange Thread Media. First is our SALT team, where we produce gatherings and resources to equip and inspire the creative potential of those in the local church. Second, we have our online stock media division where we sell visual resources for anyone in live events (from church services, to sporting events, and theatrical productions, and we even have a site dedicated to helping video jockeys specifically). Third, we have an internal live events team that provides full-service production support for events of all kinds with crew, audio/visual/lighting equipment, and creative support.

It's essential that our three different teams find ways to collaborate. When we do this, we create synergy. When we work together as a collective team, and not just three smaller divisions, we see opportunities to multiply our efforts. If there's an opportunity to help another division out, we always try to do that. And the same will hopefully work out in return. If you're in need of some assistance, then you'll gain from another team.

When you collaborate beyond your own department, you will appear better to those outside the organization. I've found in our company that the more we cooperate across our teams, the more effective we become. It's never the purpose of collaboration, but it's always the outcome. When teams collaborate within an organization, it increases their potential and momentum. Knowing what others on your team do to contribute to the mission and vision (something you would learn in a collaborative environment), you'll know what to do if they ever have to step out, step down, or move on from their role. A team with momentum is able to pick up where one left off without affecting the outcome of a project, product, or organizational property because they are a team who knows how to support another area other than their own.

**Third and finally, we must see industry-wide collaboration**. For far too long, we've allowed

#CreativePotential    171

competitiveness to stop us from making a dent in the culture because we limit our focus to our own organization and companies. For the most part, your vision is bigger than selling a widget or getting someone to come to your gathering. So what does it look like to call that "competitor" down the road and see how you can start collaborating?

SALT conferences would not exist if it weren't for a multitude of people who caught our vision and chose to collaborate with us. In turn, we take time at every gathering to pay tribute to the people, brands and ministries who have helped us along the way. It's part of the process of growing. Some may call this brand alignment or even a complex marketing strategy, but I see it as creative biblical industry collaboration.

When you take your most unique abilities and use them in a way to enlarge the vision, mission, and values of an entire industry, you get dangerously close to reaching your maximum potential. Because you are an excellent and unique contribution multiplied by the efforts of not just your own department and your own company, but countless individuals across several organizations. That's the power of multiplication and that's the potential impact of collaboration.

Let me warn you, this isn't as easy as calling the company down the street and asking them to join your vision. You've got to invest into what they're doing first. You need to find ways for both to benefit from the collaboration.

I have no idea where the saying first came from, but the proverbial quote "No one cares what you know until they know you care" is exactly why collaboration on this level will be the toughest of all. You have to show others that you want to help them and their vision before they will trust that you care about the entire industry's growth as well.

Some of you may be thinking this isn't possible. Your boss will never go for helping your competitor grow because it's essential for your organization to achieve its goals and stay in business, right? But there's another proverb that relates: "A rising tide raises all boats."

Practically speaking, if the industry grows, your customer base grows too. We can't collude with other businesses to try and create monopolization—that's against the law. But we can legally be helpful to one another and support each other by harnessing a collaboration rooted in authentic desire to help them reach their potential too.

## For You

I'd like to propose something. To best accomplish this spirit of collaboration, we need to adopt a "for you" mindset. For too long, people have seen the church, and particularly Christians, as a group of people who are "against" everything. In fact, our culture at large is even known more for what someone is "against" than what someone is "for."

Take the 2016 presidential election for example. A Pew Research Center survey identified why people voted for a specific candidate. The number one reason people voted for Donald J. Trump was that "he was not Hillary Clinton." And the number one reason people said they voted for Hillary Clinton was that "she was not Donald J. Trump."[21]

If a presidential election was decided because people are more "against" something than they are "for" something, then our world needs more of our collaborative spirit. It's time for the Church to be known more by what we're "for" than what we're "against." What if we could change the narrative and become a group of people who leverages our unique excellence in a way that's truly collaborative and let people know we're really *for them*, not *against them?*

Here are just a few examples of what being *for* others looks like:

- A *for you* mindset increases the potential of others in the community because they want to see everyone win.

- A *for you* strategy is focused more on creating solutions that help people rather than creating cool things that reflect them well.

- A *for you* budget sees creativity as an investment in your community's well-being and growth, rather than just a cost in the organizational budget.

- A *for you* person is known by many to be an advocate rather than the antagonist who is never impressed.

- A *for you* culture makes it easier to collaborate than compete.

- A *for you* leader sees people as your purpose, not just a part of your process.

- A *for you* mentality is more concerned for what's best for everyone else, not what's better than everyone else.

- A *for you* community increases the odds of winning because a true win is only possible when someone else wins.

The more we're *for* one another, the more we become like Jesus to our community. God was so for us that He sent His own Son to die on our behalf. He wants the best for us at the cost of everything else. I believe true collaboration is effective at every level because it's the model God laid out for you and me.

When we shift our mindset and see God as one who gives gifts to His children for the distinct purpose of helping others find their way back toward Him, we unlock the eternal potential we were destined for at birth. We become a collaborative force for good in the world. A force that's unstoppable.

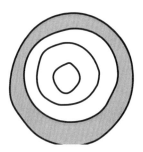

# Contagiousness: Going Viral

By now we've established the core of uniqueness, identified how to become excellent, and found a collaborative community to multiply our efforts. At this point we're at the last layer of our proverbial Gobstopper. Now it's time to change the world.

As creatives, we are wired to make a difference. We are operating at our complete potential when God is using our giftedness to impact those around us.

Let me warn you: transforming the world around you may not look like leading thousands of people to the Lord every year like a Billy Graham, or bringing millions of smiles to children around the world like Walt Disney has with his imaginative and creative empire. For most of us, we want to see our calling become a transformative agent to help at least one person move closer to God.

That's fulfilling the great commission, seeing our craft reach someone else with kingdom impact.

It's time for us to talk about contagious creativity, the fourth layer of our metaphorical Gobstopper of creative potential. It's the outermost layer because it's the thing that touches the world around us. Contagious creativity moves us from creating in context to creating on mission.

Our world has never been this ripe with opportunity for our gifts to have a profound and lasting impact. Think about it: we're experiencing "kairos" in the world today.

Kai•ros (n):
1. A right or opportune moment in time.

2. A time when conditions are right for action.

Roll that word around on your tongue for a bit. Pronounced ki-rōs (with a long "o" sound where you hear the letter "o" distinctly). As weird as the word kairos may be, it's perfect for describing the creative season our culture is experiencing.

Never has content, media, and art been consumed by a generation at the rate we're seeing today. And it increases every year, which means there's an unprecedented opportunity to be contagious with our creative calling.

Think about how much media you consume in a day. I'm talking about television, social media, Hulu, Netflix, YouTube, blogs, radio, audiobooks, podcasts, movies, magazines, music, news, etc. Do you have a number in your head? Okay, now double that number. Experts argue that a person consumes twice as much content than they perceive they consume in a given time period.[22]

CONTAGIOUSNESS: GOING VIRAL

As those who form visual, artistic, and creative works, we're poised to see our mediums carrying messages more than any other medium in the world. The opportunity before us is using our medium to be a carrier of the greatest message ever told. Before anything can gain mass appeal and change the world, the opportunity for global distribution and rapid consumption must first exist. You and I, as unique creative beings, hold the keys to seeing God perform radical transformation and supernatural revival in our world.

But it's not enough to just create. Creating without purpose adds noise to an already noisy world. Our creativity needs to cut through the noise with stories or ideas that will resonate with God's lost children and point them back to heaven. What makes contagious creativity different from noisy creativity? Contagious creativity can move people to think differently, help people see Jesus more clearly, and begin the transformational process of one's life for eternity. If our creative expressions don't do one of these things, it will merely add more noise.

## Let's Go Viral

Have you ever walked into a meeting with your boss, your pastor, or another leader in the organization, and they use the phrase, "Okay, let's create something that goes viral"? Odds are good someone in the room will bring up the fact that no one can force something to go viral. And rarely do the things that go viral start with a plan to go viral. This means the best way for something to never go viral is to expect something to go viral.

Victoria serves on our team at SALT. One of the ways she expresses her love for people is teaching fifth-grade Bible studies at her church. If you know Victoria at all, you know she's one amazing teacher. She's highly creative and has a way of breaking a subject down to a concept that is easy to understand because she is contagious with her gifts.

She once shared with our team about a conversation they had in this Bible study about what her fifth graders wanted to be when they grew up. As they went around the group, they each started to share their dreams. A few kids said they wanted to be doctors, one an athlete, and another an engineer. However, one dream stood out in particular and took Victoria by surprise as several other children began to agree.

That dream was to be a YouTube celebrity!

How amazing (and scary) is that? The generation that's in fifth grade right now recognizes the power of contagiousness so much that they want to be YouTube celebrities. As if being the most popular person in the world is the goal of life.

The odds of getting something to going viral are virtually zero percent. Half of all YouTube videos have fewer than five hundred views, and only one-third of one percent (0.33 percent) have more than a million views.[23] And most experts say that a video must see somewhere in the ballpark of three to five million views in a one week period to be considered "viral."[24]

Therefore, thinking we can control whether our creativity gains mass appeal that it impacts millions and millions of people is another lie fed to us by Satan. Viral isn't up to the creator of the content; it's up to consumers of the content.

Every time I read Acts, I see a pattern of flourishing in the way the church grew in the early days. You see story after story of the apostles preaching the word of God, and the message spreads through villages all throughout the region. As it expanded, people began to believe. It happens in almost every chapter of the book of Acts.

Just as I found in my own journey of pursuing the call from God, I don't believe this rapid expansion is a direct result of the *doing* of the disciples. There's more to it than that. The Holy Spirit was breathing on the works of this group and using their voice, their teaching, and ultimately their whole unique selves to make them a conduit for the message of Jesus.

Just as Acts 2:47 says that the *Lord* added to their numbers daily, we must recognize that it's God who does the work on our behalf. Looking to another New Testament book gives us a little more insight into this concept.

In 1 Corinthians, Paul talks about how our desire to follow specific people often leads to divisions in the Church. Essentially, he urges those in the churches of Corinth to avoid the celebrity-like attention being given to some of the ministry leaders. Within this message, we see this gem:

> "What then is Apollos? What is Paul?
> Servants through whom you believed, as the
> Lord assigned to each. I planted, Apollos
> watered, but God gave the growth. So neither he

who plants nor he who waters is anything, but only God who gives the growth."[25]

Did you catch that? Those who water and those who plant are nothing! Contagious creativity exists most when we recognize our inability to do much outside of the presence of God and the activity of God. I didn't truly step into my own calling in life until I realized that God cared far more about who I was becoming, rather than what I was doing. This is when creativity becomes contagious for the kingdom of God.

Maybe this scripture will help us see the role that we play in the message-carrying vision of the great commission. It also may help us see for ourselves that a watered-down message isn't needed to appeal to the masses. God takes care of all of that as we step into the unique, excellent community around us and desire for God to use us as impact makers in our culture.

## The Language of the Invisible

Creative works, more specifically visual arts, have a unique way of communicating across languages. In many ways, art can transcend language barriers and communicate when common dialect isn't present. While there may be exceptions based on cultural differences, art is a multilingual form of communication.

As creative beings, it's important to realize that you and I possess the opportunity to leverage this language in communicating to the world. But to use it, we must first learn it. Learning how to speak this language will come

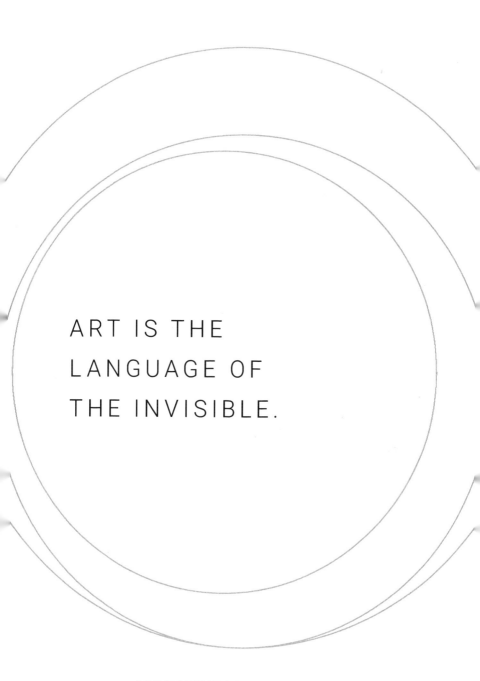

ART IS THE
LANGUAGE OF
THE INVISIBLE.

#CREATIVEPOTENTIAL

as we build our relationship with the Holy Spirit. For we do not control the language of art, God does.

Art is the language of the invisible. It can speak to us both individually and simultaneously. Art is powerful. Art is intimate. It's this invisible language that the Holy Spirit uses to move people through your creative works. The same piece of art may speak to you and me completely differently, but still move each of us in a powerful manner. That's the power of the language of the invisible.

This new language reveals a few things about the contagiousness of our creativity. First, we recognize that our creativity isn't merely for the sake of beauty but for communication. Our creations, the things we make and the projects we engineer, aren't just to be marveled at.

Truly contagious creativity tells a story. It reveals a message. It evokes wonder and awe.

Second, our creativity will be used by the Holy Spirit. Since creativity is the language of the invisible, I think the Holy Spirit will transform our creativity, when used for the purposes of expanding the kingdom, to speak in personal ways to our audiences. You and I don't have that much control over how an audience will receive our creative works. We only have control over how we present or display those creative works. So invite the Holy Spirit into your creation process and recognize that the language of the invisible will move people closer to heaven in the process.

Finally, we must recognize that our call is to advance a message, not a medium, which means our creativity isn't just a collection of ideas to spark wonder and awe but to become a conduit for life altering truth. The way we become great conduits with our creativity is to focus on the great commission and the great commandment. When we get to a place where people notice the things we're creating, be careful to not promote the medium you used but the meaning behind the message. When excellent artists begin to be noticed in culture, we recognize that we have a platform to make a difference. And those who believe in message over medium see that influence is a gift from God and is to be well-stewarded.

When you begin your creative journey, it starts as a hobby. My prayer for those who are still in the hobby state is that you see creativity as more than just pixels, pigments, particles, plans, and processes and instead see it as potential to affect the future of the eternal kingdom.

The next stage of our journey comes when our regular practicing of our craft becomes a habit. My prayer for those in habit state is that you won't let yourself think that creativity is entirely up to you and that you would invite the Holy Spirit into your creative process.

And lastly, for those who come to the final stage of our creative journey, you enter a holy state. My prayer is that God continues to establish His position as King in your heart as He continues to pour more of Himself into you, and your passion enters this holy state to make Him known more than some medium or method.

When we see ourselves as contagious creatives, we allow our creativity to transcend beyond our own abilities. We move from hobby to habit to holy, and we turn from adding more noise to finding ways to let the Lord transform those around us through our giftedness. Then and only then do our gifts and talents become living sacrifices to the Lord and our lives become acts of worship to God.

## A Vehicle for the World

For most my life, I've lived and breathed technology. I'm not sure where the passion or the interest for technology originated from, but a few years ago at Easter I discovered it may have been more hereditary than I once imagined. I was sitting with my eighty-five-year-old grandfather (to me, he's "Papaw") in the kitchen, and he was playing with his brand-new iPhone 5.

Now think about that for a second: how many eighty-five-year-olds do you know who know what an iPhone 5 is, let alone own and use one daily? For Papaw, he wasn't just comfortable using one, he had read the entire iPhone User Guide front to back.

Hold on. I've owned an iPhone since the very first iPhone was ever released in 2007, and I didn't even know they had user guides and manuals! Sure enough, my Papaw did, and he knew it inside and out. As we sat at the table together, he was educating me on some of the revelations he uncovered within the pages of the iPhone manual.

The weekend came and went, and before long Papaw was headed back home to South Carolina.

The next time I saw him, I noticed he was driving a brand-new Lincoln MKZ Hybrid. And it took me by surprise because his other car hadn't been more than two or three years old. So naturally, I asked him about it. "Hey Papaw, I love the new car! When did you get it?"

To which Papaw responded, "Thanks Luke! Just picked it up last week." Before long he started listing some of the features like the hybrid engine, heated/cooled seats, adaptive headlights, rear view camera—the list went on. However, there was one feature that stood out more than the others. This new car was equipped with a technology called SYNC. Essentially SYNC ties in with an iPhone to do voice commands, phone calls, and music, all with the audible command through the car's stereo. It was Siri before she existed.

This wasn't common in all cars, but his Lincoln MKZ Hybrid included it, and it was burning inside me to know the truth. So I asked, "Papaw, is SYNC the main reason you got this car?"

You could see him light up, to which he responded, "Yes! I had read about voice control and Bluetooth pairing in the manual of my new iPhone at Easter and started looking for the car when I got back home!"

Just as you may be laughing, so was our family when Papaw said this aloud to all of us. Who buys a car because it works with an iPhone? I mean, most people would buy a phone to work with the car they drive, not a car to work with the phone they own.

And then it hit me. If my grandfather can let a tiny piece of technology like his iPhone affect the vehicle he may drive for the rest of his life, then maybe the technology in our lives can become the vehicle God uses to affect someone's life for eternity.

The tools we use can become vehicles for others to encounter God. This is when our art transcends our own abilities. It's when our technology precedes us. And this is when our creativity becomes truly contagious.

Some may see you as a magician who comes into a meeting and pulls an idea out of the hat. Others may see you as a mad scientist who always knows how to make something happen with the push of a button, after you've been tinkering with the plan in your own private laboratory. Regardless, you carry the weight of a powerful language, which will speak in ways you'll never understand and be a vehicle to transform their lives.

The more we see opportunity through the lens of heaven, the more we will create with a perspective of eternity. As you begin to see the way this final layer of the Gobstopper comes into being, I hope you'll see what

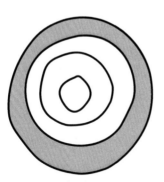

it took me years to find, that God delights in the being rather than the doing.

It's not up to you or me to move people with our art. That's the symphony God delights to be the conductor of. He doesn't need our art, the world needs our art. As we willingly acknowledge that God is the one who determines viral impact, we'll find ourselves working like it's up to us and covering our work in prayer knowing it's up to God.

If instead we choose to be like the fifth graders in Victoria's class who want to be YouTube celebrities when they grow up, we exchange the prophetic power of our creativity to become a service provider for the world's desires. And we step out of line of the Galatians 1:10 ministry model where Paul writes: "Am I now trying to win the approval of human beings, or of God? Or am I trying to please people? If I were still trying to please people, I would not be a servant of Christ."

We get a choice to be servants of the living God or servants of people, trying to appeal to popularity and the applause of the masses. Personal gain is fleeting when we've been promised an inheritance in heaven. Creativity with a heaven-minded perspective has a legacy that's eternal. And our lives intersect with the greater story of God's redemptive purposes in the world.

Our craft is most prophetic when we bring the mystery of heaven into ordinary circumstances and our creativity becomes contagious.

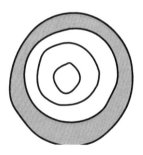

## CHAPTER FOURTEEN

# Becoming Contagious

One of the reasons becoming contagious is so critical is that it distinguishes us from cultural creativity. When people benefit from the purpose of your creativity, it adds value to their lives. As I stated in the previous chapter, it may even be the vehicle God uses to lead them to eternal life.

So far, I've followed a pattern of unpacking the philosophies of the various layers of our Gobstopper and following it up with a process of achieving this principle. However, it would be foolish for me to say "this is how you become contagious" after I've just said in the previous chapter that this is entirely dependent on your relationship with your Father in heaven. There's no way we can play puppeteer with the Holy Spirit when it is the language of the invisible that art embodies.

Therefore, this chapter won't be a series of processes to become contagious but rather a display of what being contagious looks like. I hope to show you the fruit of a contagious creative so you'll be able to identify when you are truly stepping into contagious creativity.

There is, however, a process of becoming contagious. And it only comes from letting your creativity originate from the overflow of love you have for Jesus Christ. That's it. There's no shortcut to this process. If Jesus is real to you and lives at the core of your purpose in life, and you know that He alone is the way to the Father and eternal life, then and only then does your calling have a chance of becoming a conduit of heaven's eternal spirit.

As you may remember from Act I when I told my story, it was only after I was willing to give up my creative calling in exchange for a relationship with Jesus that I became a contagious change agent for the kingdom. I'm glad God allowed me to continue using creativity as my medium of carrying His message. And I pray the same for you as you willingly lay down your own desires for the desires of Jesus to invade your heart.

## Corner or Conduit

Using creativity to point people to Jesus can be implemented a few different ways. Most specifically they can be placed into two primary categories: a corner and a conduit.

When we use creativity as a **corner**, it becomes a marketing gimmick to lure someone in. This is the tactic most seen in Hollywood or theatrical productions. It leverages all the power of great storytelling, technical innovation, humor, compelling music, and/or compulsory copywriting to lure someone in. Then at the last moment, the viewer or person experiencing the creative medium must take a hard right turn for the ulterior motive or message.

Most of us have probably seen a "faith-based film" before. Without poking fun at any one specifically, they're all using creativity as a corner to get people to Christ. In almost every one of these films, they tell a compelling story; characters overcome impossible circumstances, a team defeats all odds to win a game, or a student must convince their classmates that God is real. But then at some point there's a meeting in a prayer closet, a come-to-Jesus moment at a kitchen table or a worship service, and the film seems to take a ninety degree turn to incorporate the gospel message or salvation prayer into the storyline. If you're like me, you cringe every time this happens. The result: a cheesy film. I can't imagine how weird these "corner moments" are for those who don't know Jesus.

Then you have movies that are based on biblical stories and produced by mainstream studios, like the movie *Noah* (produced by Paramount Pictures). It was not a corner-creative approach because there wasn't a hidden message. And it did more for the conversation of the Bible in mainstream culture than any Christian-produced film in recent years. Many recognized that it took a few creative freedoms and departed from true biblical accuracy, but it wasn't a bait-and-switch mentality like most other faith-based films. This is a great example of how corner-minded creativity limits the potential by limiting the contagiousness.

This same principle is true outside of the world of filmmaking. Maybe it's an opener to an event, a song, the way we communicate to our community, or any other medium of creativity. Regardless, we must avoid corner-minded creativity. In doing so, we sacrifice the contagious element of creativity and limit our potential. On the contrary, creativity should be a **conduit**. A direct path to communicating the grace, love, truth, and hope that is found only in Jesus Christ. Not the carrot-and-stick attraction method of corner-based creativity.

I don't know if you've ever taken the time to install a piece of technology in a new building, but often you will need to run power or cable through the walls. You do this most effectively by utilizing a *conduit*. By definition, a conduit is a long hollow cylinder to carry a substance from point A to point B to avoid obstruction.

I wonder if that's the goal of the language of the invisible, to communicate in a way that avoids obstruction? Since art can be the vehicle for life change, wouldn't we want that vehicle to take the most direct path in getting people to Him? That means we must embrace the power of conduit-creativity.

Thinking about creativity as a conduit allows us to use our giftedness as a direct means of communication between those we create for and those God is calling us to reach. Conduit-creativity realizes that it's Jesus's presence that changes lives, whereas corner-creativity relies on entertainment to transform lives. Sounds like corner-creativity is more like the strategy of the world and what Taylor Swift tries to do during her worldwide stadium tours.

1 Peter 4:11 sums this concept up so well when Peter writes, "If anyone speaks, they should do so as one who

speaks the very words of God. If anyone serves, they should do so with the strength God provides."

When we step into the fullness of our potential, I hope we begin speaking the *very* words of God with the gifts we've been given. We're wasting our breath trying to add our own voice, and we become a corner to getting people to the presence of Jesus. However, when we get out of the way and allow God to oversee the doing, it allows our art and our calling to become a conduit, getting people to the presence of the one who gives eternal life without any obstruction or detour.

## Chocolate Chip Cookies

A few months ago, I was in my parents' kitchen in Atlanta, and my sister was making a batch of decadent, rich, and sweet chocolate chip cookies. They were the type you can't resist, no matter how full you are or what diet you're on. Moist, warm, and fresh out of the oven.

The way my sister makes these cookies is quite impressive. I marveled at her magician-like poise as she moved around the kitchen with finesse and ease. She knew exactly what to do and didn't need to look at a recipe. It became obvious to me she had refined this process over years of practice. She was performing as if it were her grand finale to pull these amazing cookies out of the oven at just the right time.

So I drummed up a bit of courage and asked her about this secret recipe. Maybe if she showed me how to make these cookies, I too would be able to woo my friends with this talent. When I asked her what the recipe was, I was surprised by her response. My sister didn't give me a recipe but instead threw me the extra bag of Nestlé chocolate chips.

I didn't know what she was trying to do. Was I supposed to open these for her? I thought she already put them into the mix. No, she was answering my question, but I didn't know it. Her secret recipe was just the generic recipe on the back of every Nestlé-brand bag of chocolate chips.

As I looked at the ingredients, every one of them made sense to me, except one. Salt.

Why would you add the bitterness of salt into a sweet chocolate chip cookie? Because salt enhances the flavor of whatever it's added to. Without it, chocolate chip cookies wouldn't have that rich chocolate flavor. They would taste flat.

The same is true with our own creativity. The gospel message doesn't *need* creativity, but when we add a pinch of salt, or creativity, we can enhance the essence of the gospel message.

## A Pinch of Salt

Salt isn't an acronym or abbreviation but a picture. A picture of how creativity can play a role in helping an idea or message become contagious in culture. Let me break down the four characteristics of salt and help us see a few ways our creativity can be contagious.

First, **salt is a flavoring agent**. Salt doesn't add flavor that didn't already exist; it enhances it because it's an agent of flavor. Due to the chemical nature of salt, we add it to food to bring out the elements that make food desirable for our taste buds. In doing so, we can take a bland piece of meat or an unseasoned vegetable and make it something our mouths salivate over.

We must have the same perspective of our creativity. When we're trying to be a flavoring agent with our creativity, we don't let our art steal the show. When art is in the spotlight, that's entertainment, not message enhancement. But when we enhance, we make sure that we create in a way that highlights the natural elements of whatever we're adding our creativity to. And our creative gifts become a pinch of salt in the world, acting as a flavoring agent.

Second, **salt is a healing agent**. Before modern medicine, salt was used as a common treatment for injuries, cuts, or abrasions to the skin.[26] It acted as a pain remedy because Advil didn't exist that long ago. Furthermore, people added a bit of salt to a wound to prevent it from creating additional illness as bacteria spread.

Since our creativity acts as a language that surpasses written and spoken word, our art and creative works have the potential to act as a healing agent in the world. You and I hear countless stories of people who have been burned out by religion, or hurt by church and its leaders in the past. One blog, a sermon, or a single conversation over coffee may not be enough to heal those wounds. Maybe our creativity can leverage the power of the invisible language and act as salt in a relational wound. As our creativity once again becomes a pinch of salt, we become the healing agent of wounds created by people, processes, and politics.

Third, **salt is a preserving agent**. Much like the ability to heal wounds, salt chemically removes water from whatever it's added to and slows the growth of harmful bacteria. When this happens, it prolongs the shelf life of food or other perishable goods.

As I've mentioned before, we've been commissioned to tell the greatest story in the world, but we must tell this timeless story in a timely manner that resonates with culture. When we use creativity as a conduit, we become a gospel-preservation agent in a media-driven culture. More people will be able to experience the grace and glory of our Lord Jesus Christ because of our ability to add a pinch of creative salt into our environments and messaging.

My friend Gary made a powerful statement at the 2013 SALT conference in Nashville: "Friends, we don't create for God. He does not need it. We create in response to God because the world needs it!"[27]

When we allow our art to become a response to the things God is planting into our lives, we give the world the thing they need most: an understanding of a supernatural love and eternal life. We don't use creativity or technology as an attempt to worship God as much as we use it to help others engage in worship to God and experience the presence of the Holy Spirit.

Fourth and finally, **salt creates thirst**. Because it's like a magnet to water, pulling moisture out of the things it's added to, salt naturally dehydrates. The same is true-with our own bodies. When we consume salt, it attracts all the excess moisture where the sodium has gathered, and we begin to thirst.

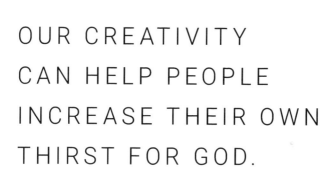

OUR CREATIVITY
CAN HELP PEOPLE
INCREASE THEIR OWN
THIRST FOR GOD.

There's no other substance I know of that will cause the body to do this, which is why it's a perfect picture for the role creativity can play in our own lives. It has the power to move people closer to God and to create a longing to be in His presence. All great art causes a thirst for more. The challenge we face is more of what? More entertainment or more encounter of the presence of Jesus?

As we leverage art to become a vehicle for change, we can use the power of salt to create thirst to let our creativity become a vessel for the kingdom. We are God's chosen people, set apart from the world and commissioned to invite people into the grand narrative of God. Our creativity, that pinch of salt added to others' lives, can help people increase their own thirst for God.

## Where Contagiousness Begins

As I close this chapter on becoming contagious I want to remind us of where contagiousness begins. It starts with a love for Jesus over all things. Just as it did in my own life, it must begin there for you too. Contagious creativity doesn't just happen. It's always intentional.

When I was touring with the Seminars4Worship conferences back in 2008, I got the distinct privilege of working with my friend, artist, and fellow VJ Stephen Proctor. Among people who know how to use visual elements to create an atmosphere where people engage in worship on a deeper level, he has refined his gift far beyond anyone else I've met.

Getting the opportunity to do all these events together that year was a real blessing for me. Not only did he and I get the chance to break bread and have insightful conversations on the role of media and creativity in the church, but I got to see him and his passion for his craft at work. There's one image he created that is forever engrained in my head that symbolizes where contagiousness starts for artists and technicians. It was a picture of a cup.

He had it so that an empty cup appeared on the screen at the beginning of the worship song. During the bridge of the song, he triggered a new clip that made it look like a stream of water was being poured into the cup, causing the cup to fill up. However, when the cup was completely full, the stream of water didn't stop. It kept going, eventually causing the water to overflow on the outsides of the cup that we'd been staring at for the length of the song.

And that's the picture for you and me on how to make our art contagious. It starts from within. As we fill our own cups and create from a position of overflow, it spills onto our art, onto our stories, and onto the technical engineering that takes place. So what do I mean by the overflow?

I'm talking about the overflow of love and passion you have for Jesus Christ. You and I can create all the art and media we want, but if we don't have the love of Christ as a well that overruns within us, we'll never truly become contagious with our creativity.

Yes, the single greatest thing you can do to improve your gift and your ability to transform the world is to do nothing creative at all, and instead fall madly in love with Jesus and His purposes in the world. As artists, we create from what's within us. Always. When the materials that we create with are full of richness and incredible value, then the art we produce will be enriched with great value.

There's a story in the Bible that shows me how time with God will visually change the way we create and share our gifts with the world around us. It's in Exodus 33 when Moses is on Mount Sinai, and God tells Moses that His presence will never leave Moses' side. Moses asks God to show Himself, and God obliges.

Only one chapter later, Moses (with the Ten Commandments in hand) walks down the mountain to share with his people all that God has revealed. And the people see a physical change in his appearance:

> "When Moses came down from Mount Sinai
> with the two tablets of the covenant law in
> his hands, he was not aware that his face was
> radiant because he had spoken with the Lord.
> When Aaron and all the Israelites saw Moses,
> his face was radiant and they were afraid to
> come near him."[28]

When you and I spend intimate, one-on-one time with God, our lives are forever changed. We become visually different, and the things we make begin to carry a weight and effectiveness that's unrivaled by anything else we can do. People will notice it, and our potential will be maximized. We're most who God made us to be when we create from the divine overflow that only He provides.

## The Completed Gobstopper

With this principle in place, we've finished the outermost layer of our proverbial Gobstopper. As we conclude this final principle, I think it would be helpful to close with a review of why this Gobstopper is layered in this manner in which I've presented them within this book.

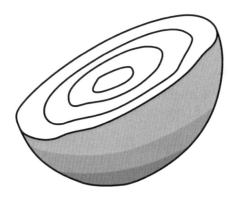

At the core, we must recognize our uniqueness comes from who God made us to be. Once we are who God intended, we have taken our first step in reaching our full potential in Christ. You'll never be able to reach your creativity potential if you're always wanting or trying to obtain someone else's creative abilities.

Next we become the best version of ourselves by harnessing the excellence God intended for our giftedness. It must come after our identity is rooted in the person and presence of Jesus Christ. As a posture of our hearts, rather than the worldly pursuit of perfection, we become a living act of worship by showing God in the good we create.

Then our gifts are multiplied through the principle of collaboration. Like iron, we begin to sharpen one another as we find ways to model Christ to one another. And in a manner only God could ordain, we increase our own potential by investing in the potential of others.

This leads us to finding a way to become contagious in our creativity, the last layer of our Gobstopper. This is the layer that touches the world, and God uses our mediums to carry the greatest message ever told to the masses. When this happens, our potential is reached because we create out of an overflow of adoration toward Christ, using our gifts as a conduit for His story.

My prayer is that you find your uniqueness and let it be the core of your creativity.

My prayer is that your measure of quality is more about heart than head, creating the good through which others see God.

My prayer is that you find a community to pour your uniqueness into, as God multiplies your abilities and talents.

And I pray for you to be contagious with your creativity, as you work from a place of continual overflow of worship.

## CHAPTER FIFTEEN

# Potential Limiters

You now know what it takes to reach the fullness of your potential in your creative gifts and unleash your God-given calling. That's a powerful piece of information to have at your disposal. But it's not going to always be sunshine and rainbows. As with anything in this world, we're going to face trials and tribulations. As the book of James begins, "Consider it pure joy, my brothers and sisters, whenever you face trials of many kinds."[29]

That's a pretty tough thing to "do" isn't it? Seeing your pain, your failure, your setbacks, and your trials as something that brings you joy? How does one delight in adversity? What does it take to find the good in the moments of difficulty? It takes overcoming these potential limiters and using them to launch back into creativity. The key is seeing them from God's perspective, not our own.

In this chapter, I'm going to walk through the five biggest factors that limit your creative potential: fear, passion, hustle, pride, and fame. None are things to avoid altogether, but with the wrong perspective and purpose, they can distract us from what God has designed for us.

## Fear: Catalytic Fuel

You need to meet my friend Elle. She and her husband live and work in New York City. And they are amazing filmmakers. In fact, Elle worked for one of the premier and most forward-thinking creative studios in New York.

This studio has won numerous Staff Pick Awards from Vimeo for some of the stunning short films they've created, not counting the number of high profile clients on their roster. Furthermore, the talent of people that work there is nothing short of exceptional. That is where fear crept in for Elle. She never thought she was good enough to make something on her own.

Elle didn't doubt she was creative—she just didn't think she was *creative enough*. And this is the cause of most of the fear that enters our creativity.

For her, the quality of work she was involved in and the people she was surrounded by created what she called a "paralyzing fear." This paralyzing fear prevented her from ever attempting to create something herself.

When you look around and see talented people operating in what seems like their maximum potential, it's tough to not focus on your own faults and areas that need improvement. This can create the same sort of paralyzing fear that overcame my friend Elle. But there's something you need to know about fear.

Fear is not a limiter. Fear can be a catalyst for greater creativity.

Fear plays an interesting role in creativity. Most people cave into its negative side and allow it to prevent them from creating. But few use it as the stepping stone to get over their own internal pessimism. At the end of the day fear is letting yourself believe that the worst-case scenario will become your reality. And that's what prevented Elle from creating.

She let the fear of not being creative enough prevent her from creating because she didn't want everyone else to think she wasn't creative, thus losing any of her input and influence with the team. Instead of listening to the whispers of God, which we've been exploring together in this second act, we tend to listen to our own conscious. And it paralyzes us from the creating that we were destined for.

Here are a few things to know about fear.

## Fear is a myth

The worst possible scenario is extremely unlikely to take place, which is why it's called "the worst possible scenario." It's unlikely that we"ll lose the job, car, house, or life savings because we choose to create. We concoct this false reality propelled by fear that we'll be excommunicated from our community because of failure—all because we create something that we feel isn't good enough.

This is all crazy talk. A community that kicks you out because of one subpar product isn't a community that was ever for you. And even if this creative "failure" becomes a reality, it will only result in a temporary loss, not a permanent effect on life.

Our world moves too fast to hold too big of a grudge against people who take creative risks. Furthermore, I believe the world around us has an immense amount of appreciation for those who take creative risks because they are heroes for so many other creatives who fight against fear. As my friend Ben Arment said about fear, "The worst-case scenario rarely happens, and when it does, it usually only impacts our quality of life, not the value of life." As beloved children of God, nothing will steal your God-given worth.

## Fear is a choice

It's in our minds and something we hold the keys to unlock. The first step in controlling this fear is to stop focusing on those paralyzing "what if" questions.

Questions like:

- What if no one likes what I create?
- What if I don't like what I create?
- What if this doesn't work?
- What if I lose all my money? My job? My reputation?

Instead, focus on the people your creativity will benefit or the positive outcomes that come from stepping into your creative calling?

- The person who your art may make whole.
- The community who may experience transformation through your craftsmanship.
- The story that will be told when you step into transparency and authenticity.
- The relational impact that may result from your creativity.

One day Elle realized that fear was a choice and decided to do something about it. She overcame her fear and created nonetheless. She found an amazing principle at work when she did. As she stepped into her own vulnerability and fears and decided to invite people in, they came from all over the place to help her.

Vulnerability beckons community. Stepping into your own potential will always cause others to lock arms with you and walk alongside you into the creative process again.

The film she ended up making is amazing! I've seen it many times. It covers an intimate and powerful subject few films have attempted to cover. Every time I see it, I can't fathom that she allowed herself to feel she wasn't "creative enough." It's better than most indie films I've seen! But it reminds me that fear shouldn't limit our potential but rather increase our potential.

## Fear is to be conquered

Both fear of failure and fear of success can be paralyzing to the creative soul. But both sides of fear are to be conquered because it requires us to rely on God as we step into the unknown. For me, the fear of not creating the right conference had to be conquered. For Elle, the fear of not being creative enough had to be conquered. And you have fears that are begging to be conquered as well.

Take Jesus for example. Imagine the fear that was before Him as He stood in the Garden of Gethsemane, begging God to let the cup pass. He was fearful of the pain He knew He had to endure to unlock heaven for you and for me. His beaten and bruised body was the last painting of grace God had intended from day one. That picture is now the bedrock of our theology and relationship with Jesus.

In this, it's certain that Jesus felt fear in His final days—the fear of what may come, but also the fear of what would happen if He didn't go through with what He needed to do. Jesus had all the power in the world to prevent the cross from happening; He was fully God and, at the same time, fully man. But He had to endure fear to become the bridge for our relational intimacy with God.

Just as Jesus conquered fear to unlock your eternal potential, you too must conquer fear to unlock your own creative potential. The best part of conquering and overcoming fear is that you'll experience in a more intimate way all that Jesus felt and knew in His final days, and you'll likely draw closer to Him in the process.

## Passion: The Fire That Burns

When I was growing up, my youth pastor was famous for saying "Keep the fire in the fireplace." He knew that a fire in the fireplace was safe and easy to contain. The fireplace was designed to provide protective boundaries to make sure the fire wouldn't become uncontrollable and spread to places it shouldn't. He also knew that if we decided to put some sticks on our parent's rug, a place that wasn't designed to protect a fire, it would burn the house down.

When it comes to our own passion, there's a fire that burns within us. It's the thing that propels us to action and gives us that drive to create more. So what is wrong with the fire that dwells deep within? Nothing, unless it's not in the fireplace God intended for it.

When the passion for what we do and the gifts God gives us begin to grow outside the fireplace they were intended for, our creativity begins to steal our worship. We were designed and purposed by God to be in relationship with Him. He is a jealous God, and nothing else is to take that place in our hearts and minds. Anything that steals God's place is what He views as evil.

John Piper puts it this way: "The essence of evil is to lose a taste for God and prefer anything more than God."[30] It's the reason Adam and Eve fell in the garden. They wanted the *knowledge of God* more than they wanted God Himself.

In the book of Exodus, an amazing thing happens. To remind you, Moses was called to lead the Israelites out of slavery and into the Promised Land. During this journey, a cloud covered them by day and a fire lit the way by night. Being in the desert, this was a very practical way of knowing God was on their side; they were provided with cool shade during the heat of day and warm light at night.

Furthermore, their campgrounds were at the base of the mountain God was living on. God was their neighbor. And in one famous moment in Exodus 32, Moses came down from meeting with God and found the entire community had built a golden sculpture out of all the materials they had in the camp. Talk about an art project!

They were so hungry to worship, the tribe united to make a golden calf so they could bow down and worship something. And in worshiping something, they built a fire outside of the fireplace and let their passion steal their worship from God.

We too make idols like the golden calf, and our passion becomes our worship. Our art should be an instrument of worship, not the object of worship. So you and I must be careful to not fall more in love with the gifts God has given us than with the Giver of all gifts.

This tends to happen when we get more opportunities to leverage our gifts. What starts as something small, an opportunity to serve, turns into entitlement. I should warn you though, entitlement always starts somewhere and seemingly grows at an exponential rate. It may seem like a simple regular opportunity, but eventually grows to a platform or position you've come to expect to have. When anything becomes the desire of your heart more than being in the presence of God, you've found your own golden calf.

Passion is an incredible thing. And when our passion is aligned with the four principles we've talked about and a healthy realization that it's God who does the *doing,* we're in a great place to use it as a powerful tool to fire us up! However, when our passion turns into something unhealthy, it's a fire that burns outside the fireplace God intended. We limit our potential because we lose sight of contagious creativity, and we become the center of our own desires. The potential is gone, and our passion overshadows our purpose.

## Hustle: Fast or Fast?

The world tells us we need to hustle to get where we want to go. And there's nothing wrong with a healthy drive to make the most of the gifts God gave us, but at some point, the hustle builds a habit that prevents us from reaching our potential. I find it interesting that the world's definition of fast is in stark contrast to how the Bible uses the same word.

Our culture defines fast by the speed at which we move; God defines fast by the process of giving up our desires to rely on His provision. What if part of our creative habits involved a regular process of hitting the pause button instead of always trying to operate at the hustle speed that seems too romanticized in today's culture?

Our church recently went through a spiritual fast together. In preparing us, one of my pastors spoke at length about the purpose of a fast. During that sermon, this quote stood out: "We don't fast to give up something; we fast to gain something."

What if God doesn't want us to be so concerned with speed but instead obsessed with relying on His supernatural presence? Maybe it's time to rest in His providential creativity.

When we fasted as a church, I didn't expect all that I would gain from it. I gave up Netflix, television, video streaming, and ultimately any online content. The result was amazing. I realized how much more aware I was of God's presence when I wasn't so consumed by other people's content.

In giving up, I gained the world as far as creative ideas and relational intimacy with God, and ultimately I think I found my potential again when it comes to my calling. In fact, it was during that season of fasting that most of this book became a reality, and God spoke into these very pages.

When we run at hustle speeds, we put our trust in the wrong thing. We are telling ourselves and others that our own ability is the key to reaching our potential. But you and I already know that one of the four layers of our creative potential isn't hustle. Speed isn't a factor for God as much as heart is.

Scripture tells us in 2 Peter 3:8-9:

> "But do not forget this one thing, dear friends:
> With the Lord a day is like a thousand years,
> and a thousand years are like a day. The Lord
> is not slow in keeping his promise, as some
> understand slowness. Instead he is patient with
> you, not wanting anyone to perish, but everyone
> to come to repentance."

God doesn't operate on our timing. Even though His time is different from ours, scripture still reminds us that the Lord is not slow in keeping His promise. His promise is to use you to fulfill His purposes in the world, which means the sooner we can get on His timing, the sooner we'll understand the potential He has in store for us.

Resist the urge to move at an unhealthy speed in working to achieve success. The problem with hustle is that it's addicting. And it will steal the margin you desperately need to be successful. I know all too well what happens when we get caught up in doing and not being. Hustle is a limiter of your God-ordained creative potential. Protect margin. Honor your rest. Keep the Sabbath as part of your creative process.

## Pride: The Craftsman's Conundrum

For some, the mere desire for excellence will limit our potential. We didn't talk about this during the becoming excellent chapter because of its potential to limit. But alas, it's time to talk about the *craftsman's conundrum*.

Craftsmen are those with incredible focus on their creative calling whose work becomes more of an art than a communication vehicle. You are a part of a tribe of artists who want to make the most beautiful things in the entire world. You struggle with the biblical definition that excellence is not the pursuit of perfection because, as a craftsman, you strive for perfection in everything you do. Every little detail is obsessed over; the slightest flaw garners painstaking agony. In the end, you'll do whatever necessary to make it right.

If you're a craftsman, you're among the best of the creative class. Unfortunately, you choose to work alone far more than with a team, likely because you see other creatives as roadblocks to the best possible outcome.

These highly capable people always see the tiniest flaws in a project. They throw themselves at their work. They don't quit until the deadline arrives or they believe the final product is perfect.

Craftsmen face an inevitable conundrum: the focus on excellence in their work causes them to never be satisfied with the result. That lack of satisfaction leads to burnout, or worse—depression. We find ourselves wanting to throw all our good gifts out the window when things don't go as planned. In our craftsman-like habits, isolation is inevitable because other creatives aren't good enough for us either.

As I've searched my own heart and processed my own tension with the craftsman's conundrum, I've realized it's a pride problem.

Pride is the root of the craftsman's conundrum because we believe we can do things better than everyone else, including God. We don't trust someone else to create as well as we can. So we shut everyone else out and do the work ourselves.

Pride kills creativity one way or another and limits us from reaching our potential. What's more, it will separate us from the love God intended for us to encounter. James 4:6 says, "God opposes the proud but shows favor to the humble."

I don't know about you, but I don't want to be in opposition to God. Allowing my pride to prevent collaboration with God seems to be the greatest potential killer of all. I'd rather be a seemingly weaker artist on the same side as God than a seemingly stronger artist without Him.

God is the Craftsman of all craftsman because He created you and me. But even God gives up the desire to control, and He modeled this for each of us. In Genesis 2, God lets Adam have dominion over naming every living being.

I wonder if God gave up control to Adam because He recognized that letting others create, even though Adam was nowhere near as creative as God, is part of the relational element of creative community. Therefore, we must walk in humility with the conundrum that lives within many of us in the creative community as well, not letting our pride get the best of us.

## Fame: Empires and Platforms

Lastly, our own fame may be the thing that steals our potential. It's weird to think about if you're just getting started on your own creative journey, but speaking from experience, our perspective gets out of place when we believe that fame is for our gain.

I recently had the opportunity to see Hillsong United during a stop on their Empires tour. For those who may not know Hillsong United, the songs they write have been sung by millions around the world. It's likely their songs have been sung more than any other artist to ever walk this planet. You have likely sung one of these over the years: "Oceans," "Mighty to Save," "From the Inside Out," "With Everything" or their more recent "So Will I (100 Billion X)."

There are countless Hillsong albums and probably thousands of songs, and in the world's eyes, they've had incredible success. You can imagine the kind of fame a guy like Joel Houston, lead worshiper, has when he steps into an arena of ten thousand to twenty thousand people. As with all creatives who have a bit of fame, it's easy to think that fame is because of something you've done. As much as you may think that Hillsong is out to make a name for themselves, I want you to know what Joel said in the middle of their worship set.

While he was sitting at the piano, Joel paused and said this about our platforms and their purpose: "For some crazy reason, God wants us to bring attention to ourselves and build a platform so we can become a platform for His purposes in the world."[31]

You see, Joel has a perspective that I long for on most days—recognizing that my success isn't so I benefit but so that God can build a platform for His purposes in the world. I believe this is the tension many touring musicians face every day, and the tension you and I get invited into as well. What do we do with the fame we may gain, as our art becomes truly contagious and begins to impact the people around us? We get back up, realizing we never deserved that platform, and leverage our influence for the sake of the kingdom.

SALT Conference isn't for me alone; it's for those in the church to recognize their potential with the gifts and talents they carry in their lives, which means my art and creativity aren't for me either.

All creativity is worship to God. As I've written throughout this book, when we create, we embody the creative characteristic of God. And when we create in a season of our unleashed creative potential, our lives become constant postures of worship, and God is most known to others through the things we create.

When our uniqueness comes out of the wrong perspective, we begin to think our platforms are for our own purposes. And that's when fame limits our potential. Those who leverage the amount of influence God has given them for kingdom purposes are those who maximize their own potential, for they have found divine confidence in their calling.

ALL CREATIVITY
IS WORSHIP
TO GOD.

#CREATIVEPOTENTIAL

# SO WHAT?

When I first moved to Nashville, I attended Fellowship Bible Church for several years. Whenever one of the pastors came to the end of the sermon, he always ended with a moment he called, "So what?" The purpose was to create a moment of reflection before rushing back into the busy lives we all have, neglecting to hear the whispers of God in our lives.

During the "so what?" no one said anything. The pastor stood at the pulpit in silence. I found that clarity always came to me in these moments because I allowed my mind to absorb all that I had just received during the sermon. And throughout the years I found the "so what?" moment was when God spoke most loudly and allowed for very personal and practical application.

As we come to the end of this journey together, it's only fitting for you to have your own "so what?" moment. For some, it may mean getting a journal and reflecting on the principles of uniqueness, excellence, collaboration, and contagiousness. For others, you're ready to dive deeper into scripture on a specific layer.

I don't want you to finish this book and rush back into the *doing* mindset. That's what killed me in discovering the destiny God had in store for me. And I wonder what sort of destiny He's inviting you into.

## Parable of the Dinner Party

There's a parable Jesus teaches in the book of Luke that fits where we find ourselves as we come to an end. I particularly like how Eugene Peterson phrases some of this story, so I've pulled from *The Message* translation:

> "For there was once a man who threw a great dinner party and invited many. When it was time for dinner, he sent out his servant to the invited guests, saying, 'Come on in; the food's on the table.'
>
> "Then they all began to beg off, one after another making excuses. The first said, 'I bought a piece of property and need to look it over. Send my regrets.'
>
> "Another said, 'I just bought five teams of oxen, and I really need to check them out. Send my regrets.'
>
> "And yet another said, 'I just got married and need to get home to my wife.'
>
> "The servant went back and told the master what had happened. He was outraged and told the servant, 'Quickly, get out into the city streets and alleys. Collect all who look like they need a square meal, all the misfits and homeless and wretched you can lay your hands on, and bring them here.'
>
> "The servant reported back, 'Master, I did what you commanded—and there's still room.'
>
> "The master said, 'Then go to the country roads. Whoever you find, drag them in. I want my house full! Let me tell you, not one of those originally invited is going to get so much as a bite at my dinner party.'"[32]

You and I have been invited into the greatest dinner party with Jesus. After receiving His invitation, we've turned Him down because of all the other priorities in our lives. We become so overwhelmed by the tasks of trying to unlock our potential that we miss a moment with Jesus to enjoy a meal together.

Here is Christ, preparing a feast for us, and we turn Him down because we have a deadline to meet or a new tool to learn. We come up with any excuse that seems more important than it is. In essence, we're just like each of these invitees.

Some of us are saying no to God because we're like the first invitee and just acquired some new land. For us, this means we have a new project that just landed and a sea of deadlines lurking. Maybe it's a new church campus we need to open or a new marketing piece to promote a new product, and the joy of the new thing causes us to turn down the invitation of a lifetime.

Or we're like the guy who turned the master down because of the oxen he needs to take care of. As creatives, our oxen are the tools and techniques we utilize. Maybe we feel the pressure to learn a new trick of the trade, a new technique, or a new form of technology. Therefore, we see that our desire to become better causes us to turn down the invitation to dinner with the King.

Then there are some of us who are like the third guy and just don't see time with God as something of importance at all. He used his new marriage as an excuse and put his own pleasure above the opportunity to spend time with the master. For you, it may not be family but those things for which you feel responsible, the things that dominate your schedule and prevent you from spending time with God. In the end, it's an inverted priority list where the wrong things aren't the right things, and it gets the best of us.

Overall there's a principle in this passage that has impacted me powerfully: Jesus wants to be first. Not first after our calling. Not first after our helping other people. Not first after ministry or our opportunity to impact the world. He wants to be first above everything. Not because He wants to limit our potential, but rather because He's more in love with us as we are, than what we should, would, or could become.

The amazing thing I've found is that the closer I get to God, the more He pours into me. And as He pours in, I am more apt to live in the divine overflow I always want to live in.

You are the most valuable thing in the entire world to God.

I fail to recognize this all the time. Deadlines never cease. A client needs something right now. I need to stay up-to-date on the newest technology or I'll be out-of-date. Or I simply don't maintain enough margin in my life to spend time with my Creator. And every single time, I deny the invitation God has handed to me.

## Back to Where It All Began

I want to take you back to where we started . . .

The day I heard God's call on my life
wasn't out of the ordinary. The voice of James
Earl Jones wasn't present, telling me to do

something. In fact, there wasn't a single audible word. When God speaks, your heart and soul know who's speaking. That call would soon bear fruit and eventually change the outcome of my entire life. And I would recognize my potential as I created out of the divine overflow in my life.

I take us back to the very first paragraph of this book, so we can see the faithfulness of our God as we come to the end. It's likely you won't hear an audible voice from God either, but your heart will know when He is speaking. And when you step into the destiny He has for your life, you too will reach your potential as you begin creating in the season of the divine overflow. In the overflow, Christ is the center of everything, and the cross becomes the perspective you create from, rather than toward.

There's likely an urgency within you to put this book down and begin working on whatever God is whispering over you right now. There's likely a desire within you to start (if you haven't already) working on the call in your own life. And it's likely that you're eager to start *doing* something.

Well, I have some advice as you finish these last few pages. Don't just do something. Stand there.

It's the reverse of the statement you're used to hearing. But as I reflect on my own "so what?" moment, I'm reminded the *doing* is what set me off course. My *doing* wasn't in line with my *being*. It was the *not doing*, just standing in Atlanta for those few weeks, that allowed me to find the true calling God had purposed for me.

So instead of putting this book down and immediately jumping into your own doing on your calling, would you consider just taking a moment to breathe? Would you allow your mind to rest so you can hear the whispers of God in your life? As you hear these whispers, I believe you'll find the voice of truth, and all your insecurities will begin a slow fade. You'll find what it means to create out of an overflow, and one day you'll find yourself walking in the potential God designed for you to operate within.

So don't go *do* anything right now. Just be.

Allow the God of the universe, the Creator of all creativity, the Provider of all purposes, pour His wisdom, will, and wonder into your life. As He does, it overflows onto your being and you'll find yourself unleashing the God-given calling on your life as you step into the fullness of your creative potential.

I pray you're able to listen.

To listen for a whisper from God.

A whisper with an amazing invitation.

Inviting you to become salt in your local community.

Salt that is unique, excellent, collaborative, and contagious.

# Acknowledgements

I dedicated this book to the few that serve on our core team. They are my real heroes. People who were willing to jump into the boat with me and sail down the river as it changed at every curve, not knowing what was before us. Katie, Nick, JoeAngel, Sarah, Caitlin, Tim, Dan, Bo, Stephen, Taylor, Jonathan, Dan, our interns and of course Victoria. Each of you hold this vision with hands open and your own creative gifts have helped craft environments for a multitude of people to find their creative potential.

I especially want to thank Katie Strandlund. Without you, this book would not be what it is today. You were the first person I told about SALT (the conference), and you were the first person I invited into this project. Thank you for caring enough about me, to say the second act needed to be rewritten. You've helped so many with your God-given calling. Those gifts may seem like ripples in the moment, but they manifest into waves by the time they hit the shore.

To the countless speakers who have poured themselves into a SALT gathering. To the companies and individuals who have invested so much into this community. To the hundreds of volunteers who have sacrificially served to help make our conferences welcoming. To you – I'm incredibly grateful. You're time and energy has created a refueling station for those in creative ministry.

I have immense gratitude for my mentors Andrew, JT, Gary and Nathan. Each of you have loved, encouraged, pastored and helped shape the creative potential in me. Thank you for constantly pushing me to be more of who God has made me to be and nothing more. I also want to say thank you to my pastors Henry and Alex Seeley. Your step of faith in starting The Belonging Co helped me find my tribe. Alex, God used a message you gave to reconfirm the SALT vision when I was on the verge of burnout.

More than anything, I have so much gratitude for my family. My mom and dad have served at every SALT Gathering since this vision was placed in my heart. They have shown me what loving people really means. They've shown me how to be the face of Jesus through service in ways I've never imagined being shown. They've sacrificed so much, for people who will never know them. And they did it for the sake of eternity. I love each of you dearly, and thank you for your support. Thank you also to Matt, Jenna, Sarah and Evan who have supported this calling by encouraging and praying for me along this journey. I'm glad to be weird with each of you in the McElroy family. I can't forget to thank my Papaw, Tom Wood. He's been a rock to our family, and his legacy is love. He's has invested so much wisdom into my life, allowing me to reach the fullness of my creative potential. For all of them I'm incredibly thankful.

Lastly, I want to thank the One who died in my place; Jesus Christ. Because you died, you unlocked my freedom to pursue the calling you had for me. That final act on the Cross has allowed me to find my creative potential and given me purpose in my process. A purpose that far exceeds any human desire; a purpose that longs to point people back to the One who changed my life.

# Endnotes

## Chapter 2:

1. Andy Stanley, *Visioneering: God's Blueprint for Developing and Maintaining Vision* (Colorado Springs: Multnomah, 1999), 63.

## Chapter 3:

2. Exodus 4:20

## Chapter 4:

3. Psalm 90:17, ESV

## Chapter 5:

4. Genesis 22:9-12

## Chapter 7

5. Opendorse Website, "Top 100 Highest-Paid Athlete Endorsers of 2016," Opendorse.com, June 29, 2016, http://opendorse.com/blog/2016-highest-paid-athlete-endorsers.

6. Colossians 1:15-17, ESV

7. Glenn Packiam, "Prophet or Provider", Keynote, SALT Conference, Nashville Tennessee. October 22, 2014.

## Chapter 9

8. Colossians 3:17

9. Colossians 3:23

10. 1 Corinthians 12:31b

11. "The QSR 50," *QSR* magazine, August 2015, last accessed September 7, 2017, https://www.qsrmagazine.com/reports/qsr50-2015-top-50-chart.

## Chapter 10

12. Tuskegee University website, "List of Products Made from Peanut by George Washington Carver," last ac-

cessed September 7, 2017, https://www.tuskegee. edu/support-tu/george-washington-carver/carver-pea-nut-products.

13. TigerWoods.com, "Health & Fitness: Tiger's Daily Routine," archived on the Internet Wayback Machine, last accessed September 7, 2017, http://web.archive. org/web/20090614045344/http://web.tigerwoods. com/fitness/tigerDailyRoutine.

14. Travis Wright, "7 Things Warren Buffett Can Teach You About Leadership," Inc.com, November 7, 2014, https://www.inc.com/travis-wright/7-things-warren-buffett-can-teach-you-about-leadership.html.

15. Gloria Mark, Daniela Gudith, and Ulrich Klocke, "The Cost of Interrupted Work: More Speed and Stress," SIGCHI Conference on Human Factors in Computing Systems, April 6, 2008, https://www.ics.uci.edu/~g-mark/chi08-mark.pdf.

## Chapter 11

16. 1 Corinthians 12:4-11, ESV

17. Scott Belsky, *Making Ideas Happen: Overcoming the Obstacles Between Vision and Reality* (New York: Penguin, 2010), 20.

18. Proverbs 27:17, ESV

19. Ed Catmull, "How Pixar Fosters Collective Creativity," *Harvard Busines Review*, September 2008, https://hbr. org/2008/09/how-pixar-fosters-collective-creativity.

## Chapter 12

20. Jon Marcus, "Bike Skill: How to Draft," *Bicycling*, March 31, 2014, https://www.bicycling.com/training/bike-skills/bike-skill-how-draft.

21. Abigail Geiger, "For many voters, it's not which presidential candidate they're for but which they're against," Pew Research Center, September 2, 2016, http://www. pewresearch.org/fact-tank/2016/09/02/for-many-vot-ers-its-not-which-presidential-candidate-theyre-for-but-which-theyre-against/.

## Chapter 13

**22.** Lancaster University, "How we use our smart-phones twice as much as we think," *ScienceDaily*, October 29, 2015, www.sciencedaily.com/releases/2015/10/151029124647.htm.

**23.** Dan Frommer and Kamelia Angelova, "Chart of the Day: Half of YouTube Videos Get Fewer than 500 Views," *Business Insider*, May 20, 2009, http://www.businessinsider.com/chart-of-the-day-youtube-videos-by-views-2009-5.

**24.** Megan O'Neill, "What Makes a Video 'Viral'?", *AdWeek*, May 9, 2011, http://www.adweek.com/digital/what-makes-a-video-viral/.

**25.** 1 Corinthians 3:5-7, ESV

## Chapter 14

**26.** Eberhard J. Wormer, "A Taste for Salt in the History of Medicine," *Science Tribune*, March 1999, http://www.tribunes.com/tribune/sel/worm.htm.

**27.** Gary Molander, "Thoughts on Creativity", SALT Conference, Nashville Tennessee. October 21, 2013.

**28.** Exodus 34:29-30

## Chapter 15

**29.** James 1:2

**30.** John Piper, "The Ultimate Essence of Evil: The Majesty of God, the Triumph of Christ, and the Glory of Human Life," sermon delivered at Passion 2017, Atlanta, Georgia, January 3, 2017, http://www.desiringgod.org/messages/the-ultimate-essence-of-evil.

**31.** Joel Houston, message from "Empires Tour", Freedom Hall, Louisville, KY, July 28, 2016.

## Chapter 16

**32.** Luke 14:16-24, MSG

# About The Author

Luke McElroy is the founder of Orange Thread Media, the parent company to SALT Conferences, TripleWide Media and Orange Thread Live Events. Through his leadership at Orange Thread, their work has been seen around the world through American Idol, Blake Shelton, Catalyst Conference and the countless of churches who have been impacted by an experience created by Luke and his team. Luke was recognized as a leading entrepreneur in his industry by being named one of the top innovators in the church by *Worship Leader Magazine* and being included on *Empact 100's* list of "Entrepreneurs to Watch Under 30." Luke has written two other books, *The Wide Guide: Blueprint for the Multiscreen Movement* and *Environmental Projection: The Collision of Modern Technology and Sacred Spaces.* He is proud to call Nashville, Tennessee home.

**LukeMcElroy.com**
**@LukeMcElroy** *on all social platforms*

# Free Resources
# from SALT Conferences

Looking for additional resources for creative ministry? SALT wants to equip and inspire you to reach your creative potential. Our free resources were created to help you with your daily workload. By visiting our free resource portal, you'll find lyric templates, event planning checklists, design software shortcut cheat sheets, filmmaker resource and more! Head over to SALTCommunity.com/free-resources to download all these amazing and helpful resources!